THE COMPLETE GUIDE TO
DRYING FOODS
AT HOME

Everything You Need to Know About Preparing, Storing, and Consuming Dried Foods

Terri Paajanen

THE COMPLETE GUIDE TO DRYING FOODS AT HOME: EVERYTHING YOU NEED TO KNOW ABOUT PREPARING, STORING, AND CONSUMING DRIED FOODS

Library of Congress Cataloging-in-Publication Data

Paajanen, Terri, 1971-
  The complete guide to drying foods at home : everything you need to know about preparing, storing, and consuming dried foods / by Terri Paajanen.
    p. cm.
  Includes bibliographical references and index.
  ISBN-13: 978-1-60138-602-1 (alk. paper)
  ISBN-10: 1-60138-602-8 (alk. paper)
  1. Food--Drying. 2. Cooking (Dried foods) I. Title.
  TX609.P237 2011
  664'.0284--dc23
                          2011039007

Printed in the United States

PROJECT MANAGER: Melissa Peterson • mpeterson@atlantic-pub.com
INTERIOR LAYOUT: Antoinette D'Amore • addesign@videotron.ca
PROOFREADER: C&P Marse • bluemoon6749@bellsouth.net
COVER DESIGN: Meg Buchner • meg@megbuchner.com
BACK COVER DESIGN: Jackie Miller • millerjackiej@gmail.com

Printed on Recycled Paper

A few years back we lost our beloved pet dog Bear, who was not only our best and dearest friend but also the "Vice President of Sunshine" here at Atlantic Publishing. He did not receive a salary but worked tirelessly 24 hours a day to please his parents.

Bear was a rescue dog who turned around and showered myself, my wife, Sherri, his grandparents Jean, Bob, and Nancy, and every person and animal he met (well, maybe not rabbits) with friendship and love. He made a lot of people smile every day.

We wanted you to know a portion of the profits of this book will be donated in Bear's memory to local animal shelters, parks, conservation organizations, and other individuals and nonprofit organizations in need of assistance.

– Douglas & Sherri Brown

PS: We have since adopted two more rescue dogs: first Scout, and the following year, Ginger. They were both mixed golden retrievers who needed a home.

Want to help animals and the world? Here are a dozen easy suggestions you and your family can implement today:

- *Adopt and rescue a pet from a local shelter.*
- *Support local and no-kill animal shelters.*
- *Plant a tree to honor someone you love.*
- *Be a developer — put up some birdhouses.*
- *Buy live, potted Christmas trees and replant them.*
- *Make sure you spend time with your animals each day.*
- *Save natural resources by recycling and buying recycled products.*
- *Drink tap water, or filter your own water at home.*
- *Whenever possible, limit your use of or do not use pesticides.*
- *If you eat seafood, make sustainable choices.*
- *Support your local farmers market.*
- *Get outside. Visit a park, volunteer, walk your dog, or ride your bike.*

Five years ago, Atlantic Publishing signed the Green Press Initiative. These guidelines promote environmentally friendly practices, such as using recycled stock and vegetable-based inks, avoiding waste, choosing energy-efficient resources, and promoting a no-pulping policy. We now use 100-percent recycled stock on all our books. The results: in one year, switching to post-consumer recycled stock saved 24 mature trees, 5,000 gallons of water, the equivalent of the total energy used for one home in a year, and the equivalent of the greenhouse gases from one car driven for a year.

Dedication

I want to thank Michael Wilson for all his backbreaking work expanding the garden this year, and his patience while I experimented with more fruit leather recipes. Another thank you goes to my daughter Emily, who enjoyed my new fruit leather recipes.

I also wanted to thank all the individuals who helped out by providing their personal stories with drying foods. They provided an important contribution to the book.

Table of Contents

Chapter 12: Dried Food Recipes and Mixes 241

Chapter 13: Cooking Raw Food with a Dehydrator 261

Chapter 14: Crafts and Other Uses 273

Introduction

Before moving to my current five-plus acre hobby farm, I had been an on-and-off vegetable gardener for more than 20 years. Because my cooking skills were less than stellar, I also needed a simpler way to preserve my various harvesting successes. I never gardened a lot during any one year, so I never learned any of the more complicated and time-consuming traditions such as canning. I eventually discovered dehydrating as a way to help preserve fruits and vegetables.

Over the years, I have tailored my drying routines and have done some dehydrating with just about everything I have grown, as well as used the dehydrator on store-bought produce when the occasion to do so strikes (such as after a big sale at the grocery store). I will soon be tackling new recipes for dried meats and jerky, as well as doing more experimentation with cheeses.

This book is a collection of my own personal dehydrating knowledge along with a great deal of research to create a valuable handbook for the novice or even for someone who already has some food-drying experience.

Dehydrating food is a simple task, but you do need to know a few things about the process and technique in order to dry your food successfully.

There are many reasons why you might choose dehydrating, such as the ease of storing food once it is dry, the low cost of dehydrating, and the quality of the results compared to some other storage methods. You also can save money by dehydrating at home as well. It is a simple process that will not require a steep learning curve, and you can get started without having to spend any money on equipment if you wish.

This book has been broken down to explain the general ideas of dehydrating food for storage and then by the particular types of food (herbs, fruit, vegetables, meat etc.). Each chapter has a list of common foods of that type with specific treatment and drying time information. You can find some recipes for using your dehydrated foods in each chapter, too. There is no sense in drying it if you cannot use it afterward. A chapter on dehydrators will fill you in on all the details for when you decide to invest a little bit in a proper machine for your food drying.

Interest in drying food has been growing, as more people are looking for wholesome, organic, and natural foods again. This is leading more families to go back to doing their own gardening and looking for easy ways to preserve what they are growing. Dehydrating foods fits the bill.

Chapter 1

BASICS OF
HOME DRYING

Before we start looking at specific techniques and recipes for drying food, you first need to know a little more about what it all entails.

A Little History

Though it may seem that drying food for storage is a novel idea, it has been around for centuries (certainly longer than freezing or canning). Native Americans often dried strips of meat or fish out in the sun to create jerky, and they dried berries, corn, and squash to save them for long winter months. When Europeans took to the sea, the men would take many dried provisions with them to last the months between resupply stops. As settlers worked their way across the new United States, dried foods were important as a way to preserve crops for the winter.

These are just a few examples of how people have been drying foods for thousands of years. If it was good enough for our ancestors, it surely is good enough for us. This extensive history also proves that you can dry food without special or modern equipment.

Dried Foods Today

Today, people do use dehydration around the house for food preservation, although not as frequently as in the past. There are few other areas where dried food has become important in the modern world.

Dried cranberries

Those of us old enough to be familiar with the early space program probably associate dried foods with astronauts. Although most dried foods that went up into space were actually freeze-dried, they do still rely on standard dehydrated foods for storage while at the International Space Station today. These foods can be stored for long periods without any additional power being used, and they are extremely light. Dried fruits and jerky are common as snacks because they can be eaten without rehydrating.

The military has been using dried foods for some time as well to create rations for soldiers that are light to carry and will not spoil. The MRE (Meals Ready to Eat) is the most common example and still is used frequently today. MREs contain dehydrated meals such as spaghetti with meat sauce, chicken fajita, meatloaf, and jambalaya (depending on the menu for the year). You can see that dried food has been a significant part of our past as well as our current culture.

How Food Dehydration Works

The basic premise in food dehydration is to remove as much moisture as possible in order to make the food inhospitable for any harmful bacteria, fungus, mold, or mildew. All of these need moisture to survive, and they will not be able to infect your food if it is too dry for them to live.

In order to take all the moisture out, you need to expose your pieces of food to warm moving air. The heat causes the water to evaporate, and the air then draws away that moisture. Dehydrating using only one or the other (heat or air) may work, but it will take much longer and might leave you at risk of your food starting to spoil before it is dry enough to be safe.

And spoilage is always a possibility if you are trying to dry your foods in less than ideal circumstances. Commercial dehydrators and ovens typically will work just fine to dry out your food safely, but there can be risks of spoilage if you are using air drying or sun drying. *There is more on these specific methods later in this chapter for more details.* Any food can start to spoil if the drying takes too long; so, you need to plan your dehydrating so that it is completed in a short period.

Why Home Dry?

You might be wondering why you should use drying as a way to preserve and store your food. It is not as common as freezing or canning, so why do people dry their foods in the first place? Actually, there are several good reasons why you would want to go this route.

Cost savings

One important aspect of using home drying is to save money. There are several ways you can stay frugal by drying or just by preserving your own food in general.

Buying in Bulk

When something is on sale or in season, you are going to want to buy lots of that item in order to maximize your savings. Unfortunately, that does not always work well if you are buying any kind of perishable goods. So, having an easy way to preserve your purchases for later use means you can take advantage of that sale by buying a large quantity.

Another aspect of "bulk buying" is that you often can get better pricing when you buy larger quantities even if they are not on sale. That can mean shopping at a warehouse store (such as Costco® or Sam's Club®) or even just buying packaged food in larger containers. Either way means a lower cost for you as long as you are able to properly preserve it all for use later. There is no sense in buying a ton of any food product if it is going to go to waste later.

Reducing Food Waste

And speaking of wasting food, this is a cost-saving benefit all on its own. By drying perishable food on a regular basis, you will find you have less waste due to spoilage than if you try to use it all at once. Of course, that depends on how much food you buy in the first place, but a good storage routine helps a great deal with waste in any case.

Eliminating the Need for Commercially Dried Foods

If you use dried fruits, vegetables, or meats in your home and usually buy them that way, you can have some further savings by doing it yourself. Dried foods can be expensive, and there is no reason why you cannot save the extra cost by drying those foods at home.

Whether it is a package of dried fruit and nuts for trail mix or dried vegetables for a soup mix, you can make these things at home for a fraction of the cost of a purchased item.

Health benefits

Cost is only one factor you should consider when thinking about home drying your food. Another one is health and keeping your food as nutritious as possible.

One of the best benefits of home drying is that the slow application of heat does not destroy the vitamins, minerals, and other nutrients in your food. For the most part, the only change that takes place is the loss of moisture, so your dried food is nearly as nutritious as it was before you dehydrated it. Iron, fiber, and several B vitamins are retained with virtually no loss at all. Vitamin A will be partially lost, and you, unfortunately, will lose most of the vitamin C in your foods because it is a "water soluble" chemical.

Unlike commercially preserved foods, you will not need to add any chemicals to your dried foods. They naturally will stay preserved for months (if not years) without any additives, preservatives, or other chemicals you might not want in your food.

You also can see benefits to drying food when it comes to the taste and quality of the final product. When the water has been removed, the taste becomes more concentrated. If you are going to eat your dried food without rehydrating it first (as with meat jerky or dried fruit), you will find the flavor is much stronger than in the original form. That is why sun-dried tomatoes are such a wonderful ingredient and so different from fresh tomatoes.

Rehydrating your food by adding water again will dilute this effect, and your reconstituted foods will taste "normal" again.

Powdered Foods

Being able to make your own food powders is a good way to add extra flavor to your cooking. A custom blend of dried and then powderized vegetables (such as onions, peppers, celery, or carrots) can be used as an addition to many other dishes such as soups, stews, pasta or just about anything. Not only does this add extra taste but also a load of nutrients you would otherwise not have.

Not all dried foods will work as a powder. Some will dry to a tough leathery consistency and might not crumble well enough to make a powder. A little experimentation should show you what you could do along these lines. A blender or even a mortar and pestle are all you need to make your own powdered foods.

Compared to other preservation techniques

These are all excellent points, but it is also helpful to know how the qualities of dehydration measure up against other forms of food preservation.

When compared to the most common way of preserving food (freezing), drying comes out ahead in cost because it will not use

electricity during the entire shelf life of the food like a freezer does. You also do not have to worry about any losses or waste due to a power outage or freezer failure. Freezing might be the easiest, but there are more cost issues while the food is being stored.

The other main way to preserve food is by canning in glass jars. This method does not have any costs associated with ongoing storage like the freezer does, but there is a much larger initial investment when you start canning. Not only do you have to buy a canner, but you also need a sizable collection of canning jars along with their matching lids. The jars themselves are a one-time expense, but you will have to buy new lids for each jar whenever you do more canning. Each time you can a jar of food, the lid becomes slightly warped with the vacuum, and they will not hold a seal more than once.

Dried foods can be stored without any additional costs for containers, and there is no cost to maintain your preserved food. Overall, it is the cheapest method available.

Once dried, most foods are a fraction of their original size. This is unique to dehydrating, and it makes storage a lot more efficient compared to preserved foods by other methods. You can store more dried food in a quart jar than food that still has all its water content in place. With canning, you even have extra fluid so your food will take up more space.

In terms of health benefits, drying holds on to nutrients during processing, but so does freezing. Frozen foods are remarkably healthy once they are thawed out. Canned foods are treated at a high heat, and that can destroy some of the healthy compounds in your foods. Taste is also the same issue. Dried foods are much like their original states once rehydrated, but canned foods can be soft and bland due to the extra heat that goes into the processing. Frozen food will taste as though you were cooking fresh, or at least close to fresh.

One last comparison is the ease of processing. Canning takes the most work, with the filling of the jars and cooking each one to exactly the right pressure. Freezing is usually quick but can take time to properly package foods and to do any blanching. Blanching involves a short exposure to boiling water to kill any active enzymes in your food before drying. *There are more details on this in Chapter 6, the chapter on vegetables.*

Drying may take a long time (12 hours to several days), but there is hardly any effort to it once the dehydrator is filled up. It sits and dries on its own with no extra work, and then the food can be packaged away.

Basic Methods for Home Drying

This topic will be covered in more detail in Chapter 2, so this is only an overview to provide an introduction.

The basic premise for drying food is to expose it to a warm flow of dry air that will remove most (if not all) of the moisture in your food. That is all there is to it. It is not the same as "freeze drying," which is far more complicated and not something most people are ever going to do at home.

What is Freeze Drying?

Freeze drying puts frozen foods in a vacuum, which then draws the moisture out as the water rapidly changes from solid directly to a gas. This process removes more water than standard dehydration and creates a dried food product that can still be edible for years. Freeze dried foods are rehydrated by the addition of hot water, much like typical dehydrated food.

You can give dehydrating a shot with just your oven before investing in an actual food dehydrator, and some people stick with the oven anyway because it is handy. A true dehydrator does work better if you do not mind buying another small appliance. In some cases, you actually can use your microwave for some dehydrating as well.

Some people choose to go a more natural way and use the sun for food drying. This method has the added benefit of not using hours of electricity, though it can be hard to control and manage. This is the method used most often through history; so, it certainly can be mastered with a little practice and effort.

The bottom line is that you can go about starting a food drying routine in several ways, and by learning more about them all, you can choose which one will work best for your own needs and lifestyle. You might find that you use one method for some foods and another for something else.

No matter which method you use, there are some basic principles to keep in

Peppers being sun dried in China

mind when dehydrating. Always wash and clean anything you are going to dry. Lay your thinly sliced food out on your screens or trays, evenly and in one layer. Nothing should be overlapping. Allow a little bit of space between each piece so air can flow freely between everything.

When you go to check for "doneness," remember that foods will be softer while still warm. You may have to take a few pieces out of the dehydrator to cool before you can assess their progress accurately. This is important with heavier fruits and vegetables.

Use the guidelines presented in this book as a starting point, but always use your own judgment when dehydrating. There are always variables to consider, such as climate and humidity in the air, the ripeness of the food you are drying, and even how thinly you are slicing. Check your drying food periodically, and never leave it alone for 12 hours until you are more familiar with the process. If the book says 12 hours, you may get a shock to find over-dried food that should have been taken out at the ten-hour point. After a few sessions, you will know how things dry in your own kitchen. It is always a good idea to take notes so you can remember what worked and what did not work for the next season.

Storage Methods

Dried foods have the wonderful feature of being preserved no matter how you store them (within reason); so, you will have many different options on how to store your food. The most important feature is that the container is air-

*Photo courtesy of
Douglas and Sherri Brown*

tight to make sure damp air does not begin to rehydrate your food and add moisture back into your container.

Plastic storage tubs are excellent, and you can use glass jars with a tightly fitting lid. Because dried foods are extremely light, many people hate to use heavy storage containers if they do not have to. Tupperware®-style containers are the most common way to store your foods. You can then keep them any place that is not overly humid (basements might be a bad idea).

For short-term storage, you even can use plain paper bags. If your home has any chance of animal pests, just remember that paper is not much of a protection against teeth.

When drying large quantities of food, you can use food-grade buckets with a rubber gasket seal. These are ideal for beans or any other dried food you want to have on-hand in volume. Dried food might not seem like "real" food, but you do need to make sure all storage containers are graded for use with food. Buckets intended for paint are probably not a good idea. Even dry food can pick up contaminants from the plastic.

An additional way to protect your dehydrated food is with vacuum sealing, which removes all the air from your storage container for added security and preservation. You can buy small vacuum devices for the kitchen that can be used for this, and they can be used together with plastic bags or even glass jars. If you are going to use plastic bags, you might want to get bags designed

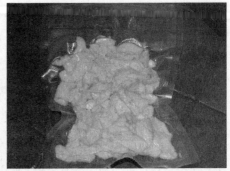

Photos courtesy of Douglas and Sherri Brown

for vacuum packing. A strong zip-close bag might suffice, but they are not designed to stay "locked" when there is the pressure of a vacuum inside the bag.

Plastic bags will collapse down to create a solid pack that is great for storage. To use jars, you have to make a small hole in the lid

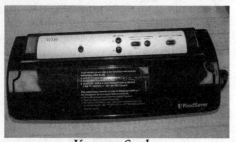

Vacuum Sealer

Photo courtesy of Douglas and Sherri Brown

that you then quickly cover up once the vacuum is achieved inside. Many vacuum sealing machines will come with seals you can use for this or at least instructions on how to do so when using jars. Because the vacuum will be broken each time you open the jar or bag, it is not a good idea to use this for any foods you will be using frequently unless you want to run the sealer every time.

When dehydrating with imprecise methods (such as the sun or oven), take one extra step before packing your food up for long-term storage. Food that you will use in the shorter term will not need this. Temporarily pack your dry foods in plastic bags and leave them in the freezer to kill off any potential bacteria. Leave them for 48 hours, and then pack as you would for pantry storage. This is called "pasteurizing" and can be done by heating in the oven, but the freezer method requires the least amount of work.

Safety with Dried Foods

The reason that dried foods preserve so well is that bacteria, fungus, or mold, at least not the types of bacteria that are harmful to humans, cannot survive where there is no moisture. Where there is no water, there will be no bacteria. This is why dried rice and beans are so ideal for long-term storage and why they last so long without any special storage conditions. You can reproduce those conditions with any kind of food when you dehydrate it to remove the moisture.

But you do need to be careful when you dry that *all* the moisture has been removed. Any pieces that are still soft or damp can add bacteria or mildew to the entire container, and you run the risk of contaminating all of your food. The drying instructions will indicate what the final product should be like. Some will be leathery, but some will be brittle and crisp. Knowing what to expect means you can judge accurately when something has been dried enough for safe storage. Let a few pieces cool off before assessing their dryness. Something like banana slices will seem soft and damp while still warm, but they will be hard once they cool down.

For any dried foods you plan to use in the near future, such as a blend of dried fruit for trail mix; you will not have to be quite so concerned about perfect drying.

What Can Be Dried?

Just about any kind of food product can be dried for preservation, though many liquids can be a challenge. This is not just a technique for herbs and fruit slices. You can dry all manner of fruits, vegetables, herbs, mushrooms, and even meat and dairy products, too.

Knowing the right length of time and temperature for drying is the key. Once you know how long it takes, you can dry any kind of food. There are no limits.

However, you do need to watch out for high-fat foods. Avocados and peanut butter are mentioned again later in the book, but they are not suitable for dehydrating because there is too much oily fat in them to dry properly. Only water and moisture can be removed, and high-fat foods are prone to going rancid, so they are not used for any long-term storage purposes.

Using Dehydrated Foods

It is fine to know how to dry foods, but you also need to know what to do with them afterwards. Dried foods are versatile; so, you have many options. Many dried fruits are eaten as is. That is, they are not rehydrated or prepared in any way. Depending on the fruit, you can just eat the dried slices as they are. Banana and apple both work well for this. Dried kale or zucchini is a little more unusual and can be eaten just as it is like a healthy chip. Fruit leathers and meat jerky also are eaten in their dried form.

For any other uses, you will have to rehydrate your food, which means to put the water back in. The most effective way to rehydrate your food involves a little heat as well as water, usually just by simmering until everything is softened up again. You can do this by itself or add your dried foods to other liquids already cooking (such as a soup or stew). With the proper recipes, you also can use dried foods in place of non-dried as long as the recipe has been adapted to include the extra liquid it will need. Otherwise, you will have to rehydrate before using it in the recipe.

Chapter 2

METHODS FOR DRYING FOOD AT HOME

Drying may seem like a simple process, but you have several options on how to do it. The fundamentals are all the same (removing moisture from food), though each method is going to have its own set of pros, cons, and other considerations. You do not have to choose just one. Some of these ideas might work in some situations, and other techniques can come in handy other times.

Sun Drying

This is the "old fashioned" method people in the past would have used the most for their food drying. It can be a little tricky for the novice though.

How sun drying works

Letting the power of the sun doing your drying for you can be an easy option if you are in the right climate for it. All that is involved is leaving your sliced foods out in the sun to dry.

Tomatoes sun drying

On average, you will need to have at least two days of hot sun, but three or four is better. If you do need more than one afternoon's worth of sun, do not leave your food outside overnight. Even if you have elaborate covered or screened-in trays, the drop in temperature will cause moisture to form back on your foods and ruin your day's drying. Always bring everything inside.

To get the most air movement in the sun, always dry your food on mesh screens rather than solid trays. These can be made at home easily with heavy-duty stainless steel screening and a simple wooden frame. The screens must be stainless steel to keep from contaminating your food (nothing galvanized). Cheesecloth might be used for smaller trays or when drying light herbs. It would not be strong enough to support much else, especially large quantities of sliced vegetables.

Benefits of sun drying

The main benefit of sun drying is the fact that it costs nothing to "run." A stove or dehydrator will use electricity while running for hours on end, but you can leave trays of food out in the sun for a natural drying process that costs you nothing at all. You may be able to use the sun indoors, near large windows, or even in a greenhouse, but it usually is done outdoors. This means less clutter in your kitchen during drying time.

With outdoor drying, you can spread out when you have a lot of food to dry. No limitations on counter space, oven racks, or dehydrator trays.

Drawbacks of sun drying

Though it is free and spacious, there are a few considerable problems with using the sun to dry your food. The main problem is the lack of control. You can set an oven to a certain temperature and trust that it will stay that way for as long as you want. The sun is not quite so accommodating. A bright sunny day can provide eight hours or more of great drying weather, as long as a cloud or a cool breeze does not move in. When the temperature drops or the sun vanishes, you usually can adjust your timing to leave your food in the sun a little longer. In the event that it gets hotter than you expect, it can sometimes mean a quicker drying period. If you happen to be out checking on your food, you will need to bring everything in, or you can end up with scorched food.

Temperature aside, there is one additional drawback: pests. Insects can be a huge problem, particularly with sweet fruit that has been laid out to dry. You also can have problems with birds or squirrels coming to enjoy the buffet you have laid out for them. A light mesh netting over the top of your trays should suffice in keeping all pests out of your food.

You also need dry weather, not just sun. If your climate is humid, then your food will not dry sufficiently no matter how hot it gets.

What Should I Sun Dry?

Which foods you should dry in the sun really depend on your specific climate, but anything that dries quickly will work best because you are not as likely to suffer from a change in the weather. The longer you have to leave your food out (two days or more), the more you run the risk of potential problems. Anything that will dry in under a day is more suitable for sun drying, especially if you are a novice at it. Foods such as tomatoes, spinach, or zucchini can all be done in a day or less.

Air Drying

Like sun drying, using just the air is a natural and inexpensive option when drying some types of foods.

How air drying works

You let the air naturally dry your food items. This is different from sun drying because you usually use air drying indoors, provided you have suitable ventilation in your home. With this, you focus on the air rather than the heat to dry out your food. Unfortunately, without the added heat, air drying can be one of the slowest ways to dry your food unless you have a particularly warm area to work in.

In the past, this would have worked well indoors if a wood stove were going. The pioneers would have been starting up the stove right when the final harvests are brought in. For today's modern family, conditions are seldom so perfect.

Benefits of air drying

As when using the sun to dry, air drying requires no special equipment and costs nothing to implement (unless you choose to run a fan to keep the air moving). It is quiet and will not be as much of a disturbance as running a dehydrator or keeping the oven door open all afternoon.

Because there is little added heat, this can be a gentler way to dry certain things that would do poorly under the heat of the sun or the oven. Herbs are best dried this way, for example, as their delicate and aromatic oils can degrade with too much heat.

Drawbacks of air drying

The main problem with air drying is the time it can take to get food dry. Mold or mildew can take hold before the moisture level drops to a safe level, which makes this a risky bet for most foods unless you have just the right conditions.

You should use air drying only for quick-drying things such as herbs, thinly sliced fruit, or vegetables. Because it is not ideal, the instructions in this book do not provide specific times for air drying.

Oven Drying

The best way to give dehydrating a start without buying any special equipment is with the oven you already have.

How oven drying works

Your oven is not specifically designed for drying food, but it can be a great dehydrator once you know how to set it. Set the temperature low (the specifics will depend on what you are drying), and let it "cook." Some oven models might not allow for a low enough temperature, as their lowest settings are often about 200 F. Ideally, you will want enough control to lower it down to 100 F.

Usually, you will have to leave the door open to let the moisture out, because the oven is not built to vent out excess water vapor.

Lay out your food on a baking sheet without overlapping any pieces. They might need to be turned over part way through because the air does not ventilate through the surface of the pan.

Photo courtesy of Douglas and Sherri Brown

Benefits to oven drying

It uses one major piece of equipment that you already own, which is why most people try oven drying at least once before going out and getting an actual dehydrator. That makes it handy and convenient, and using the oven means you do not have an additional piece of kitchen equipment to store away.

Drawbacks of oven drying

Unlike the sun, the oven does have temperature settings so you can be more precise with your drying. But the reality is that an oven is not meant to be used this way. Heat is only one half of the dehydrating equation, with air movement being the other half. And that is not addressed with an oven. You can leave the door open to help let the moisture out, but there is no real air motion inside. This can lead to food being slowly cooked without ending up dried.

Another problem is that your oven is a frequently used appliance, and not everyone can afford to have it tied up for hours drying foods. Having a spare oven can be helpful, but that is not generally an ideal option. An oven also will use quite a bit more electricity to operate compared to an electric dehydrator.

If you are doing your dehydrating in the summer, such as when strawberries are in season, having a hot oven running all day can make your house a lot warmer than you might like. Using the oven would work better for fall drying instead.

Food Dehydrators

These kitchen appliances are designed and intended specifically for the purpose of drying food. That does make them a better option because they are built for this task and handle it the best. A number of good models of varying sizes and features are on the market.

How dehydrators work

The basic premise for a food dehydrator is to produce a warm stream of moving air to dry your food. The fact that it moves the air (usually with an internal fan) is what sets this apart from just using the oven. It also operates at the right temperature.

Your sliced food is spread out on trays, usually stacked quite closely together and kept protected in a larger case. Depending on

the model, you may have temperature settings and timers to help regulate your dehydrating. Most units are about the size of a microwave, although the larger ones can be closer to bar fridge size.

Photo courtesy of Douglas and Sherri Brown

Basic dehydrators operate at about 100 degrees F to 115 degrees F and do not have controls to adjust the temperature. More sophisticated models will have a thermostat control. The instructions provided in each chapter of this book will specify what temperature to run your dehydrator for the timing provided. If you cannot turn up the heat, you will have to extend the drying time to compensate.

If you wish to increase the heat beyond what the directions state, you may reduce the drying time to an extent. But too much heat will cook rather than dry the food, so you will not want to increase the heat much higher than 130 degrees F regardless of what is being dried.

Benefits of food dehydrators

The rather obvious benefit is that a dehydrator is built for this job, and it is the most suitable option for drying food quickly and conveniently.

Simple models might not have temperature settings, which would put a dehydrator at a disadvantage compared to an oven, but even those that do not have such settings are designed to produce the low level of heat you need for drying food.

The design of a dehydrator usually involves a number of stacked trays (five, six, or more), which is a much better use of space than an oven that can only hold three racks at most. This provides a lot of drying space without using too much counter space. A dehydrator's racks are not too deep and are designed specifically for slices of food. So, you can maximize your space while still allowing for room between everything for airflow.

Drawbacks of food dehydrators

It does mean you have to buy another small appliance, which will cost a little more than just using the sun or an appliance you already have (oven or microwave). Dehydrators are one-function machines, so you will not be able to use them for other tasks around the kitchen.

They are not particularly expensive if you go with a small simple model, but a larger unit can be several hundred dollars. They are unique pieces of equipment, and if you are getting a big one, your local stores probably will not have it in stock. That means added shipping costs.

A dehydrator is not a loud machine, though it does create more noise due to the fan compared to running a relatively silent oven. It is a small drawback for the most part, unless you are hosting a dinner party in the kitchen. Otherwise, the hum is usually low enough not to be a problem.

Excalibur dehydrator
Photos courtesy of Douglas and Sherri Brown

Choosing the right food dehydrator

This can be a tough question, particularly if you are just getting involved in food dehydrating. If you have the resources, you can always start with a large Excalibur®, with ten large trays and a price tag near $300. However, until you have done a little dehydrating, you may want to start a little smaller and work your way up to the major equipment.

You will want to consider a few things, such as what you plan to dry, and how much drying you expect to do. Wanting to dry a few herbs each summer will have different requirements than a complete dehydrating system where you preserve all your food this way (both store-bought and home-grown).

If you are going to be drying many different types of food (herbs, fruit, vegetables, meats), getting a machine with a temperature setting is a good idea.

A small kitchen would do better with a smaller unit even if it means you have to dry more batches to get it all done. Your dehydrator may have to sit out for eight to 12 hours or more, so you are not going to want it taking up half your counter space for that length of time.

Microwave Drying

This may not be the first method that comes to mind when you think about drying food, but there is definitely a place for the microwave when it comes to dehydrating some things.

How microwave drying works

You simply "cook" your food in the microwave on a lower than usual setting, which eventually dries it out. Because you cannot leave the door open during drying like you can do with the oven, you will have to do your drying in short spurts and open it up in between to let the moisture out.

Benefits of microwave drying

Like oven drying, this method allows you to make use of an appliance you likely already have. It is cost effective because you do not have to buy any new equipment. Using a microwave is also fast compared to the other methods. Most foods can be dried in under half an hour of total time, which is a fraction of the time it would take in a more conventional dehydrator.

Drawbacks of microwave drying

This really is not a great method for drying food, though it will do for small batches when you are pressed for time. As mentioned above, you can not let the door stay open to vent out the moisture, which makes it difficult to get the food to dry out rather than cook. For this reason, you would only want to use a microwave for something that does not have a huge water volume in the first place. Herbs do work quite well this way, for example.

Parsley that was dried in the microwave
Photos courtesy of Douglas and Sherri Brown

Microwaves are notorious for cooking unevenly, which will make any drying task more difficult, as some parts of your food will dry faster than others, even if you slice them uniformly.

Also, a microwave is small; it will not hold multiple racks of food like a dehydrator. You only will be able to use it for a few things at a time, though the speed does mean you still can do quite a bit over the same period if you want to be in the kitchen moving food in and out of it.

Electric Dehydrator Versus the Oven

Because these two are the most common ways of doing home dehydrating, some additional points need to be made.

Both devices have adjustable temperatures and can be operated precisely (compared to the sun), but you should not assume that there is a consistent difference between the two. That is to say, if one particular food takes six hours in the dehydrator but eight hours in the oven, you cannot assume there is always going to be a two-hour difference from one device to the next. Always read the appropriate timings provided in the various chapters of this book.

The reason for this is that all foods are different when it comes to how quickly or easily they dehydrate. Some have a great deal of water in them to start with, and some have a very dense structure that prevents moisture from leaving. These two variables mean the added air movement of a dehydrator will not always be as much of a benefit with one food compared to another. Some foods will dry just as well in the oven as in a dehydrator, and sometimes it will take far longer.

The point here is that you should not make assumptions when trying one method or the other. There is no set pattern to how much longer something will dry in the oven compared to an electric dehydrator.

ABOUT YOUR DEHYDRATOR

Though several types of dehydrating methods are included in this book, most people are going to do their food drying with an actual dehydrator. So, you need to know the details on these machines before you buy or even build one.

When you think about dehydrators, you likely are thinking of the typical electric models that you plug in to operate. But if you want to use the sun for your power source, you also can have a dehydrator for that.

Electric Dehydrators

Electric dehydrators can cost you anywhere from $30 to several hundred dollars. And so, you can expect to find quite a range of sizes and features when you go to purchase one.

The less expensive models are the simplest. They usually are made up of a stack of slotted trays (four or five layers) that sit on one another with a base that includes the heating element and

fan. These types of dehydrators are great entry units, but they do lack features that can be helpful to a more experienced dehydrator.

One of the main drawbacks with this form of machine is that they do tend to

dry unevenly. You can get half of one tray (usually at the bottom) that is finished while other parts of the batch are not. As long as you are around to remove pieces as they are finished, it should not be a huge problem. Of course, it would be better to leave it for the designated time and not have to pull it apart continually.

The stacked types of dehydrators do have the benefit of being expandable. Depending on the model, you can get additional trays to make the machine larger (up to 20 trays in some cases). The fan will not get any stronger, though, which does mean the top trays definitely will take longer to dry than the bottom ones, but it is still an option. A good point about these models is that they expand upward, so they do not take up any more counter space if you add more trays.

The other main type of electric model is the cabinet type, with an enclosed cabinet or box the trays slide into. These dehydrators are able to regulate their temperature better and can be used for other things, such as making yogurt or rising bread dough, when you remove the trays. Drying is much more even with a cabinet dehydrator, and they are usually quieter when running. Because each tray slides out independently, you do not have to necessarily dismantle several trays to access the one at the bottom.

Specific makes and models

Trying to cover every possible make of food dehydrator is beyond the scope of this book, so only the larger manufacturers are listed. This is mainly for comparison purposes, so you can see which machines offer which features.

American Harvest

This is one of the best names in entry-level dehydrators, and they are sometimes referred to as Nesco® dehydrators (that is the company that makes them). All of their machines are the stackable kind, though different lines have different features. Their Gardenmaster dehydrators are the most expensive and offer the most features.

The Gardenmaster Pro has four trays but can be expanded to 30, and its adjustable thermostat runs from 90 F to 155 F. For something a little fancier, there is a digital version of the Gardenmaster Pro. Not only are the controls digital but also with a 90 F to 160 F thermostat, you also can set a timer to shut off when you are not home. That is excellent feature can help prevent overdrying. The digital model is also expandable, but only up to 20 trays. Both of these models will cost around $120, with the digital one being the more costly.

The less expensive versions are Snackmaster® dehydrators, which will run you between $50 and $75 depending on the specific model. Their Snackmaster Entr'ee is usually under $50, which makes it a popular choice for the novice. There are no thermostat controls, and this one has the fan unit on the top instead of the bottom. You will get about 400 watts of power (compared to the 1,000 watts of the Gardenmaster models). The other two Snackmasters, the Encore and the Express, do have thermostats and can be expanded from their original four trays (to either seven or ten).

The last two options with American Harvest do not have names but are models FD-37 and FD-39. They have no thermostats and only 400 watts of power. Like the Entr'ee model, they are less than $50 each.

Aside from their line of dehydrators, Nesco also has several good accessories to go with their machines. You can buy additional trays to stack your machine higher, and they have both fruit leather sheets and finer mesh screen sheets that you can insert onto the trays for easier drying. If you want to use your dehydrator to make jerky, they offer a kit that comes with an extruding gun, spices, and instructions.

Excalibur

Excalibur is a well-known name in dehydrators, and they make high-quality machines. All of their machines are the cabinet variety and so cannot be expanded. They currently have four-, five-, or nine-tray models available. You should note that the trays are considerable larger than the trays in a stacked model. For costs, the four-tray model is just over $100, and you will be paying at least $200 for the others.

The big difference in cost between the four-tray and the five-tray can be attributed to the added features. The four-tray version is a basic dehydrator with less power than the larger models. It has 220 watts of power and thermostat settings, while the five-tray can give you 440 watts of power, and the fan is larger. So there is more difference than just the number of trays.

The five-tray version has a thermostat to control the temperature and comes in a version with a timer and auto shut-off (up to 26 hours). You get these same features in the nine-tray models, but there is also more power with 600 watts. The nine trays provide about 15 square feet of drying space.

Like American Harvest, Excalibur also carries a line of accessories. They have nonstick leather sheets and jerky tools, too.

L'Equip®

Not as well known as the others, the L'Equip machines are also worth looking into. They only have three varieties, and they are all stackable styles. Their smaller model is under $100 and has four trays of dehydrating space. The motor is 500 watts, and you can control the temperature between 93 F and 153 F. It can be expanded by adding extra trays (up to 12).

Their largest model is around $160 and has six trays. They have a unique twist by offering two deep trays with four regular ones to accommodate unusual items such as a loaf pan or large flowers. This model also comes with fruit leather sheets and yogurt cups (for making yogurt rather than drying it). It comes with six trays but can be expanded up to 12, and there is a timer and thermostat control.

The L'Equip machines are rectangular and narrow compared to the Excalibur, so they do take up less counter space.

Weston®

Weston dehydrators are cabinet style, and they come in six-, eight-, and ten-tray sizes. For these machines, each tray will provide about 1 square foot of space, so you can figure out how much total drying space you get with each model. There are 5-inch fans in all three machines mounted in the back to blow air forward rather than up through all the trays. This can help with flavor mixing and the problem of having the bottom trays dry first.

The thermostat is adjustable and will handle temperatures between 84 and 155 F. The six-tray version has a 500-watt heater, but the other two are a bit stronger at 600 watts. Other than the size and power, all their models are the same in terms of features. You also can buy kits for making jerky that have extruding guns and special drying racks. The Westons will run between $100 and $140, depending on the size you choose.

Good4U®

The Good4U dehydrators often are compared to the Excalibur line, as they are quite similar. There are two sizes, one with six trays, and one with ten. One big difference compared to the Excalibur machines is that there is no door for the Good4U machines; the front of each tray slides in tightly against the ones above and below it. That does make access easier, but that means you cannot use this cabinet-style machine for other purposes (such as rising bread dough) because once you pull out one tray, the machine is no longer closed in.

The ten-tray model has a timer, and they both have adjustable thermostats. They also come with handy accessories, such as non-stick fruit leather sheets and a finer mesh liner for small items. The smaller unit is around $150, and the larger one will be closer to $200.

Other Manufacturers

The above companies are known for their dehydrators because they either specialize in these machines or just have a large line of them. Other kitchen appliance companies do make dehydrators that should be mentioned as well.

Salton® makes a simple stacking dehydrator with no thermostat or any other controls. It is another inexpensive way to get started while you try this out. You can find Salton machines at many department stores.

You may have heard of Ronco® dehydrators because they are well known in the world of infomercials. They are cheap stacking units, and the quality is not the best. If you were going to spend the money, other models would do better.

And at the other end of the spectrum is the Sedona® dehydrator. They only make the one model, and it typically costs over $300. This unit is clearly not for a beginner. It is a cabinet machine with nine large trays and two separate fan and heating units. All the controls are digital, and you can change the temperature or set a timer that runs for 99 hours.

Choosing one right for you

With so many models available, it can be hard to choose the right one. This is doubly true if you are new to dehydrating, and you have no experience with these machines to draw on. How to make your choice?

The main thing you want to think about is how much food you plan to dehydrate. With a small garden or just the occasional de- hydrating chore, you really do not need a huge nine-tray ma- chine. A smaller one is better until you find yourself with more drying tasks than it can handle. A stackable machine will let you do some expanding, which is a nice feature until you determine your needs.

Cost cannot be ignored either. There is a wide range of potential prices, from $50 to $300. Make sure you get a machine that is within your budget, especially if you are just starting out.

Cheaper machines do tend to be louder, with cabinet models be- ing the quietest. Because there is an internal fan running all the time, there is bound to be some sound no matter what. It might not be a consideration for you, depending on where in the house you will be running it and whether it will disturb you.

Also, consider what you are going to be drying. Having a thermostat control is extremely helpful if you are going to use your dehydrator for a number of different applications. If you know you are only going to be drying vegetables, then you can forgo that and save some money.

And this is just the electric dehydrators. The next section will cover a little more on the solar varieties that might also be suitable for your circumstances.

Solar Dehydrators

If you are interested in using the sun's energy for dehydrating, you most likely will have to construct your own setup. Complete solar driers typically are not sold commercially, though you can sometimes buy plans or kits. This is going to be a bit of a do-it-yourself project.

There is more to making a solar dehydrator than just laying food out on a cookie sheet in the sun. Although that does work, you can build a much more efficient type of dehydrator to maximize your sun power when drying food. There are many ways to build a good solar food dryer, so feel free to get creative once you have a few ideas.

Electric models usually have trays that nest one on top of the next because the fan will move air through them all. A solar drier does not have that feature; so, you will want to build them so your food is spread out in one layer. This does mean that it can take up quite a bit of space.

First, you will want to make sure your food is as enclosed as possible. Cheesecloth draped over baking sheets will work in a pinch,
but it is not an ideal approach. So, you could build a flat box (as long
and wide as you wish) that has a screened-in lid to keep out debris
and insects. Inside, you could lay your food out on regular baking
sheets. This would be the simplest design for a solar dryer, and you
would only need wood, screws, and some window screening.

This type of solar dryer can be improved if you want to get fancier with your construction. Using a solid sheet to hold your food
inside is fine (and easy), but without ventilation under your food,
you will have to flip things over part way through in order to get
a decent drying. You also could consider building mesh trays to
hold the food inside your box.

Trays can be made from a simple wooden frame with screening
through the middle. You can use window screens for the lid of
the box, but you should not use that material for any trays your
food will be sitting on. It is not safe for food use. Stainless steel is
much better, although you could make small trays with cheesecloth bottoms instead. However, trays made with fabric might
sag once you put food on them.

With these mesh trays, your overall dehydrator box needs to be
a little larger to accommodate space underneath the trays. Otherwise, it will work the same.

These approaches are great for ventilation but are not as good for
heat accumulation. If you live in a cooler climate, you can further adapt your dryers to help heat things up a little more. The
best way to concentrate the heat for drying is to change the lid
from mesh to glass. This does make construction a little harder,
although you can often use old wooden framed windows to make
things easier.

A glass lid will keep the heat inside, but as you are trying to dry food rather than cook it, this can also be a problem. When using glass this way, you must have lots of side and/or bottom ventilation to keep the air moving around your food inside the box. If you are particularly handy, you could even incorporate a solar-powered fan inside to get the air moving.

These are just some concepts and ideas to get you thinking about how to build your own solar dehydrator. For a good collection of designs, plans, and ideas, read *The Solar Food Dryer* by Eben Fodor. There are actual construction plans within this book that will get you going.

If you really do not want to build your own unit, you can experiment with solar dehydrating with a hanging mesh dehydrator from Food Pantrie. These five-tray units are completely enclosed in mesh to keep insects out and to allow for air ventilation. They look a little like hanging closet organizers. Although they do a fair job, they are not designed to expose your food to the sunlight well. They are a good choice for a starter unit or to dry things that do not require heavy heat (foods that dry in just a few hours).

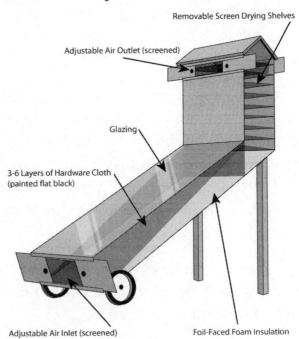

Removable Screen Drying Shelves

Adjustable Air Outlet (screened)

Glazing

3-6 Layers of Hardware Cloth (painted flat black)

Adjustable Air Inlet (screened)

Foil-Faced Foam Insulation

Sample design of a solar dehydrator

Chapter 4

DRYING HERBS

This is one of the easiest places for someone to start learning about how to dry foods. It might not be the most common place to start (people tend to start with fruit), but it really is the simplest.

Herbs are fine in texture and have little water in them to start with compared to a slice of a juicy strawberry, and they will dry up quickly. Dried herbs are so common around the kitchen that you will not have to go out of your way to think about

ways to use them. They are a good example of how flavors are intensified with drying, and fresh herbs that you dry yourself are even more flavorful than store-bought dried herbs.

Dried marjoram

Preparing Herbs to Be Dried

Many people grow their own herbs, but you definitely can take advantage of drying your own even if you are getting fresh herbs from the store.

Harvesting herbs

This step is for the folks with their own herb gardens. The specifics on how and when to harvest will vary from herb to herb, although most can be harvested as soon as they are large enough to lose a few leaves or sprigs without killing the plant. Also, depending on the herb, you will want to collect leaves, stems, and/or seeds as well. You can just pluck leaves off, but it will do less damage to the plant if you use a small pair of scissors or shears instead.

To speed up your drying process, try to harvest herbs after a day or two of dry weather rather than after a recent rain. If your herb garden is inside, hold off watering for a day before harvesting for dehydrating. Do not be tempted to let your plant dry out, even if you plan on harvesting the entire plant. When starved of water, the plant will draw moisture (along with the aromatic oils) from the leaves into the stems and roots of the plant. You can end up with bland-tasting leaves if you dry herbs from a desiccated plant.

When you are harvesting, remember how much an herb will shrink when dried: far more than what you see with other foods.

A few handfuls of an herb might mean a tablespoon of final dried herb. On average, you can expect 8 ounces of fresh herb material to become just about 1 ounce of dried product.

Cleaning and preparing

Once you have picked your herbs, remove any dead leaves or excess stem pieces you do not need in your final dried herbs. If you are drying an herb in seed form (such as dill seed), remove the seeds from the rest of the plant and take off any extra husks or seedpods. Herbs with small leaves are best left on the stems and will come off much easier after drying than before.

Dry any excess moisture off the herbs by gently pressing them between a layer or two of paper towels.

Methods for Drying Herbs

Due to their light nature, they are ideal for nearly any type of drying. You can really choose whatever works best for you. For nearly any kind of herb, you need to dry them completely until they are crisp and crumble apart easily.

Sun drying herbs

Sun drying might actually be too harsh for some herbs, but that will depend on the climate and weather where you are. Hot summer sun can dry herbs extremely quickly, and the heat can destroy the finer oils that give the herbs their unique taste and smell. If you are going to dry outdoors, keep your trays of herbs out of the direct sun. Even set them out in the shade if you can. In a sense, you are aiming for more of an air drying but with some of the sun's heat added in.

When laying your herbs out, take care to place them so the leaves or pieces cannot blow away once they start to dry out. Dried herbs are light and will take off easily in even a slight breeze. Keeping them under a layer of mesh or screen can make things much easier.

Air drying herbs

Herbs are the best suited for air drying, even indoors. The traditional way to dry herbs would be to bundle them up (leaving the leaves on the stems for easy handling) and hang them from the rafters until they were dry through. By doing this in a brown paper bag, you will keep your drying herbs safe from dust and insects though it will take a little longer if you keep them under wraps like this. A bag will also catch any dried leaves or pieces that break off as they dehydrate. Just poke a few holes in it to help the air move around.

On average, your herbs will be done in a week or two using this method. The slower and cooler process is best to preserve the flavors of your herbs. Specific times for this method are not provided because it is imprecise.

Dehydrating herbs

A dehydrator can work well with herbs providing it does not get too hot, or you can end up with the same damaging situation as you would with sun drying. Your dehydrator should be no hotter than 110 F for the best results.

One thing to remember when using a dehydrator with herbs is that they have intense aromas, and the inside of your dehydrator is fairly confining even with the fan running. So, unless you want your basil to taste more like rosemary, you probably should keep your herbs separate. Of course, if you are drying herbs to be mixed together in a blend later anyway, you do not need worry about this.

You also will find that drying herbs this way will have a strong smell through your kitchen, which might not be suitable if you are doing other cooking at the same time. A kitchen that smells heavily of garlic or basil can have a negative effect on your cookies or cake.

Depending on your herbs, you likely will have finished drying your herbs in less than eight hours. You just need to lay out a single layer of herb pieces on each tray of the dehydrator and let it run.

When drying any herbs that are in seed form (dill, coriander, fennel), the small seeds may fall through the holes in your dehydrator trays. Stainless-steel window screening can be used to line your trays, and it is food safe, or you can use a layer or two of fine cheesecloth.

Oven and microwave drying herbs

The oven is too warm to do herbs decently, and it should be avoided as a drying method unless you can set it down to 110 F. The microwave, on the other hand, can work well with herbs. You want to place a single layer between two sheets of paper towel on a plate. Run the microwave on about half (or medium) power for two minutes, and check on your herbs. If they are not dry, continue to microwave them for 30 seconds at a time until they are dried through.

Storing Dry Herbs

Dried herbs are usually stored in glass jars to protect them from air exposure, though any kind of opaque container will also keep the sunlight out as well. It just needs to be sealed tightly.

You do not want to store any dried herbs in paper containers or bags because the added exposure to air quickly will make the herbs go  stale, not to mention what the aroma in your storage room would be like if all your herbs were packaged this way.

Regardless of the container, label them clearly because it can be hard to tell one from another once they are dry.

Specific Drying Instructions for Herbs

For the most part, the process and details of drying individual herbs are going to be the same regardless of what you are drying.

Even so, there can be some variation in temperature and timing when drying a large-leafed herb versus one with smaller, finer leaves. Here are some of the common herbs you might be drying to get the precise details. You will know when they are done because they are completely dry and will crumble apart easily.

Because herbs are used in their dry form, either as flavorings in cooking or to be brewed in a tea, there are no instructions included for rehydrating.

The instructions include a little information on how to harvest, but you can just as easily purchase fresh herbs from the store or market if you are not growing them. The drying process will be the same either way. For the most part, all herbs will be dried at a temperature of 110 F, whether in the oven or in a dehydrator.

Chives

If you are able to use fresh chives, it is recommended that you do so because the fine oils in chive leaves will dissipate quite a bit during drying. You can use a dehydrator or microwave for chives, but the sun is likely going to be too warm for these delicate herbs. Because they grow much like blades of grass, you will not be picking leaves from a stem like most herbs. Snip a couple of inches off the tops of your plants, and then chop further into ¼ inch pieces for drying.

> *Dehydrator:* Set at 110 F, four to six hours.
> *Sun drying:* Eight to ten hours, but keep them out of direct sunlight
> *Oven:* Set at 110 F, four to six hours.

Basil

Because of the heavier leaves, basil takes longer to dry than most other herbs. You can pluck the leaves from the stems before drying if you wish, or wait until the leaves have thoroughly dried to pick out the stem pieces.

> *Dehydrator:* Set at 110 F, eight to 12 hours.
> *Sun drying:* One to two days, depending on the temperature
> *Oven:* Set at 110 F, eight to 12 hours.

Oregano

When doing your own harvesting, you must pick the leaves just before the flowers open up in order to have the best-flavored herb. Dry them as quickly as you can to preserve that fresh flavor.

> *Dehydrator:* Set at 110 F, four to eight hours.
> *Sun drying:* Eight to 12 hours, kept in light shade
> *Oven:* Set at 110 F, six to eight hours.

Thyme

Make sure to blot your thyme leaves dry before dehydrating. This is one of those herbs that should be dried before trying to strip the leaves off the stem.

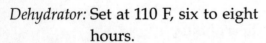

> *Dehydrator:* Set at 110 F, six to eight hours.
> *Sun drying:* Eight to 12 hours in light shade
> *Oven:* Set at 110 F, seven to ten hours.

Mint

If you are picking your own mint, choose the large leaves before the plant goes to flower. Any variety of mint can be dried, and they all have their own unique twist on the mint flavor. You can even grow chocolate mint or pineapple mint.

> *Dehydrator:* Set at 110 F, six to eight hours.
> *Sun drying:* Eight to 12 hours, kept in indirect sunlight or slight shade
> *Oven:* Set at 110 F, six to eight hours.

Rosemary

You should not wash rosemary leaves unless they are noticeably dirty, and you can pick the leaves once you notice they have developed their strong smell.

> *Dehydrator:* Set at 110 F, six to eight hours.
> *Sun drying:* Eight to ten hours in the full sunlight
> *Oven:* Set at 110 F, eight to 12 hours.

Dill

With dill, you can harvest and dry the flowers, leaves, and/or the seedpods. They all have the same flavor, although the seeds are the strongest part of the plant. If you are going to use the flowers, you have to clip them from the plant just before the blooms actually open up. You can trim off the leaves anytime and even use the smaller stem pieces as well. For the seeds, you have to wait until after the plants blossom for the seeds to form. They can partially dry right on the plant before you cut the seed heads off (be careful not to lose any loose seeds). You will need to dry the leaves/flowers differently than you do the seeds.

For the leaves, stems, or flowers:

> *Dehydrator:* Set at 110 F, six to eight hours.
> *Sun drying:* Dry whole sprigs for about two days; indirect sun is best.
> *Oven:* Set at 110 F, six to eight hours.

For the seeds:

> *Dehydrator:* Set at 120 F, four to six hours.
> *Sun drying:* Four to eight hours in open sun
> *Oven:* Set at 120 F, four to six hours.

Parsley

Besides being used fresh as a gar-nish, you can find many other uses for dried parsley. Trim the leaves off as soon as they open up.

> *Dehydrator:* Set at 110 F, six to eight hours.
> *Sun drying:* Eight to 12 hours out of direct sun
> *Oven:* Set at 110 F, six to eight hours.

Ginger

Because ginger is a thick root rather than a leafy herb, it will be a little different than the others listed. The best way to dry gin-ger is to either slice it *very* thinly or grate it. Either way, peel it first. It will grate a little easier if you use a frozen piece of ginger root. Unlike the other herbs, your dried ginger will not crumble but will come out leathery and still able to bend (pliable). There should be no moisture present though.

Dehydrator: Set at 110 F, four to six hours.

Sun drying: Eight to ten hours, and full sun is fine.

Oven: Set at 110 F, four to six hours.

Sage

Green sage is usually used as an herb, but you can dry and cook with most other sage varieties too.

Dehydrator: Set at 110 F, eight to 12 hours.

Sun drying: Ten to 12 hours, under indirect sun

Oven: Set at 110 F, ten to 12 hours.

Tarragon

Snip off young leaves, and make sure to pat them dry before getting started. You will want to harvest before your plant starts to flower.

Dehydrator: Set at 110 F, six to eight hours.

Sun drying: Eight to 12 hours in light shade

Oven: Set at 110 F, eight to ten hours.

Coriander and Cilantro

These are listed together because they are actually the same plant. Technically, the plant is coriander, as are the seeds, but the commonly used name for the leaves is cilantro. So like dill, you will have two options when harvesting and drying. Harvest young leaves for dry-

ing, with only the finest stem pieces. You can wait until seeds start to dry on the plant to harvest them.

For leaves:

> *Dehydrator:* Set at 110 F, six to eight hours.
> *Sun drying:* 24 to 36 hours, in light shade
> *Oven:* Set at 110 F, six to eight hours.

For seeds:

> *Dehydrator:* Set at 120 F, four to six hours.
> *Sun drying:* Four to eight hours in open sun
> *Oven:* Set at 120 F, four to six hours.

Bay

Though bay leaves are quite large for an herb, they are traditionally used whole (most recipes will call for one or two leaves rather than a measure in teaspoons). So when drying bay leaves, you need to take care to leave the leaves intact. You may have to break one in order to test for dryness.

> *Dehydrator:* Set at 110 F, six to eight hours.
> *Sun drying:* Ten to 12 hours, turning leaves over once after
> 　　　　　　　halfway done in direct sun
> *Oven:* Set at 110 F, eight to 12 hours.

Fennel

Fennel is closely related to dill, and the plant is used in the same way (both the leafy pieces as well as the seeds). The flavor is more licorice than dill though. Trim off the leaves when they are still small, and later you can harvest the seeds just as the seedpod starts to dry on the plant. If you wait too long, the seeds will fall off the plant and be lost.

For leaves:

> *Dehydrator:* Set at 110 F, six to eight hours.
> *Sun drying:* Eight to ten hours in shaded
> sun
> *Oven:* Set at 110 F, six to eight hours.

For seeds:

> *Dehydrator:* Set at 120 F, four to six hours.
> *Sun drying:* Four to eight hours in open
> sun
> *Oven:* Set at 120 F, four to six hours.

Garlic

For drying, mince fresh garlic cloves as finely as you can (after removing husk or skin). When minced, it might fall through the grid on your dehydrator, so use a layer or two of cheesecloth. Once dry, you can use the granules as is or run them through a food processor to make a finer garlic powder.

> *Dehydrator:* Set at 120 F, eight to ten hours.
> *Sun drying:* Eight to ten hours in shade
> *Oven:* Set at 120 F, six to eight hours.

Marjoram

Pick the older leaves once they have grown to full size (not the newly emerging ones).

> *Dehydrator:* Set at 110 F, six to
> eight hours.
> *Sun drying:* Eight to ten hours
> in light shade
> *Oven:* Set at 110 F, six to eight hours.

Chamomile

So far, these all have been herbs used in cooking. But you also can dry herbs for use in teas. Chamomile is a good example. If you are growing chamomile, wait until the flowers have opened completely before you harvest. Let them dry slightly on the plant before harvesting to quicken your processing time.

Dehydrator: Set at 110 F, four to six hours.
Sun drying: Six to eight hours completely out of the sun
Oven: Set at 110 F, six to eight hours.

Lemon Balm

Lemon balm leaves should be picked just as the flower blossoms are beginning to form but before they bloom. You can use both the leaves and the smaller stems. Chop the stem pieces for quicker drying.

Dehydrator: Set at 110 F, six to eight hours.
Sun drying: Eight to ten hours in indirect sunlight
Oven: Set at 110 F, six to eight hours.

Catnip

Although your first thought might be that you do not even have a cat, dried catnip does have other uses. Many people enjoy it in an herbal tea blend for themselves.

Dehydrator: Set at 110 F, six to eight hours.
Sun drying: Eight to ten hours in shaded sun
Oven: Set at 110 F, six to eight hours.

Recipes for Dried Herb Blends

Individual herbs on their own are great in many dishes, but you can also add more variety to your cooking with some well-chosen blends of herbs you made yourself. Most of these will include herbs you can dry yourself, although some of the ingredients likely are not going to come out of your own home garden (such as cinnamon).

The instructions are the same for all the mixes. Just combine the right herbs, and store them in airtight jars or other containers.

Italian Herb Mix

This is a great all-around mix for seasoning Italian dishes

- 2 tsp. dried basil
- 2 tsp. dried oregano
- 1 tsp. dried sage
- 1 tsp. dried marjoram

Poultry Seasoning

Use in any chicken or turkey dishes, including homemade stuffing.

- ¼ tsp. dried thyme
- ¾ tsp. dried sage
- ¼ tsp. black pepper
- ⅛ tsp. marjoram

Chicken Breading Seasoning

This is the spice mix to use if you are making your own chicken coating or breading for fried chicken. It is just the spice blend; you will need your own coating recipe to go with this.

- 2 Tbsp. dried parsley
- 1 Tbsp. dried oregano
- 1 Tbsp. dried thyme
- 1 Tbsp. dried marjoram
- 2 tsp. dried rosemary
- 2 tsp. dried ginger
- 1 tsp. garlic salt
- 1 tsp. onion powder
- 1 tsp. celery salt
- 1 tsp. black pepper
- 1 tsp. dried sage

Herbes de Provence

A classic herbal blend used in the south of France. You can use this in nearly any kind of dish. The lavender is traditional, but the flavor may be unusual for anyone not used to it. Feel free to leave it out.

- 2 ½ Tbsp. dried oregano
- 2 ½ Tbsp. dried thyme

- 2 Tbsp. dried savory
- 2 Tbsp. dried lavender
- 1 tsp. dried basil
- 1 tsp. dried sage
- 1 tsp. dried rosemary

Pork Seasoning

This blend can be used for anything from pork chops to a tenderloin.

- 2 Tbsp. dried sage
- 2 Tbsp. dried parsley
- 2 tsp. dried thyme
- 2 tsp. dried rosemary
- 1 tsp. garlic

Fish Seasoning

You can use this herb mixture on just about any type of white fish for a quick dash of flavor.

- 1 Tbsp. dried tarragon
- 1 Tbsp. dried basil
- 1 Tbsp. dried dill
- 1 Tbsp. dried marjoram
- 1 Tbsp. dried parsley

Creole Seasoning

Some of these spices will have to be store-bought, but you can use some of your home-dried herbs as well.

- 3 Tbsp. paprika
- 2 Tbsp. salt
- 2 Tbsp. garlic powder

- 1 Tbsp. pepper
- 1 Tbsp. onion powder
- 1 Tbsp. cayenne
- 1 Tbsp. dried oregano
- 1 Tbsp. dried thyme

Herbal Salt Replacement

This is a good general-purpose blend to replace using extra salt when cooking or serving food. It is similar to a few of the commercial blends you can buy.

- 1 Tbsp. cayenne
- 1 Tbsp. garlic powder
- 1 Tbsp. onion powder
- 1 tsp. dried basil
- 1 tsp. dried oregano
- 1 tsp. dried thyme
- 1 tsp. dried parsley
- 1 tsp. dried savory
- 1 tsp. black pepper
- 1 tsp. dried sage
- 1 tsp. dried lemon peel, grated fine
- 1 tsp. dried marjoram

Growing Your Own Herbs

Full growing instructions for all these herbs are beyond the scope and purpose of this book, but if you are going to grow your own for drying purposes, keep a few things in mind.

Most herbs are annuals, which means you will have to plant new seeds each year for a new crop. You can either buy new seeds every spring or allow some of your plants to develop their flowers to produce seeds you can collect.

Unless you specifically are harvesting for seeds (such as dill or coriander), you will want to prevent your plants from making any flowers and seeds because they will change the taste of your herbs as soon as seeds are formed. So, pluck off any developing flower buds as soon as you see them. Either that, or wait until the plant is ready to flower, and harvest the entire thing for drying.

Herbs can be grown in any sunny or lightly shaded area, even indoors if you have a large enough window with a table or wide sill. Keep them well watered.

Because herbs tend to be aromatic, many are naturally "insect proof" to some degree, which can make for easy care on your part. But if you do need to repel any insect pests, several excellent all-natural insect sprays work well on any plants you intend to eat. Herbs do not need to produce large roots or fruits, so fertilizer is usually unnecessary.

CASE STUDY:
PRACTICE MAKES PERFECT

Melissa Taylor
Hampton VA, 23663
www.facebook.com/bickedwitch

Melissa is a bit of an old-school dehydrator who uses sun and air drying for her foods. She has a homemade hanging rack with several trays made with recycled screens and other materials. Of course, it took a few attempts to make the best use of this type of dehydrator. The first time she dried herbs, they stuck so badly to the screens that she lost most of her batch. Not to mention that the screens all smelled like herbs when she was done. So now, when she dries anything, she layers paper towel between her food and the screened trays.

Drying at home since 2002, Melissa usually uses homegrown herbs for dehydrating though she also dries fruit on occasion and sometimes garden seeds. She grows and dries herbs to save money. And of course, home-dried herbs have a great deal more flavor to them as well. Melissa just lays out her fresh herbs and checks on them periodically until they are dry enough to crumble. When the mood hits her, Melissa also dries flowers and fruit that she uses for crafts and seasonal decorations. She gets a lot of use out of her homemade dehydrator.

She has tried bananas using her warm-air method, but the fruit flies got to be a problem before the fruit dried out enough.

Before drying, everything gets a wash in cool water and a good patting dry with paper towels. When finished, her herbs are stored in either small glass spice jars or larger stainless steel canisters.

Chapter 5

DRYING FRUIT

After herbs, fruit is the most commonly dried food for people who dehydrate at home. It is a great way to store it, and it often can be eaten while still dry (banana chips or fruit leather, for example). People probably dry more to be eaten that way rather than as a storage method.

Preparing Fruit to Be Dried

Taking a little time at the beginning can make a big difference in the quality of your final dried fruit.

Harvesting or buying fruit for drying

If you are growing your own fruit, you should pick at the peak of ripeness. Fruit with spots or holes still can be used as long as you cut out the bad parts. You are going to be slicing it up anyway. Take care to be gentle with your fruit to minimize bruising. Depending on the fruit, you might have one big harvest all at once or be able to do small batches of dehydrating through the season as you pick ripened fruit.

For drying, you will want to get fruit at its cheapest in order to maximize the savings. That means buying in season more than anything else. Many stores also will drop their prices dramatically for fruit that is getting

Photo courtesy of Douglas and Sherri Brown

overripe. For many purposes, it would not be suitable, but overripe fruit is just fine for drying as long as you are going to do your drying soon after buying.

And do not forget farmers markets as a great source for fresh fruit in larger quantities, too. Talk to the vendors if you really want to do up a large batch. They might give you additional price breaks if you buy a few bushels instead of just a small basket. Just make sure you are up to the task, or you can end up with wasted fruit.

When fresh fruit is not available, you can do some drying with canned. It might not have the same cost savings, but you can create some good dried fruit snacks just the same.

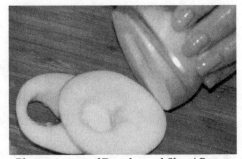

Photo courtesy of Douglas and Sherri Brown

Cleaning and preparing fruit

Depending on the fruit, you will need to peel and seed each piece and cut out any brown or damaged spots. Any fruit you are not peeling should be washed as well and then patted dry.

Fruit should be sliced evenly, about ¼ inch in thickness, but you can vary this to your own tastes and needs. Some fruits can be halved or even dried whole. It just takes longer. In some cases, the peel actually does not need to be removed but should be cut or pierced to let the moisture out. If you omit this step, your fruit will take a long time to dry. Grapes, cranberries, and blueberries are notable for this.

Additional fruit preparations

One unique problem with drying fruit is that some fruits will darken considerably when exposed to air (apples and bananas, for example). A little browning will not have any effect on the taste or quality of your dried fruit, but the final product can be a little unappetizing. You can take a few different steps to keep your fruit looking fresher. Blanching in boiling water is one option, but using a dip is the more common option when drying food because it does not add as much extra moisture.

An acid-based dip will stop the enzyme action, and you can do this in a few ways. The easiest is a commercial product that comes as a powder. You just mix it with water as per the instructions and give your fruit slices a short soak. You can use a few home-made solutions. Crushing vitamin C tablets and dissolving them in water can make an ascorbic acid dip. A good dip can be made with about five 500 mg strength tablets in a ½ quart of water. Ascorbic acid powder also can be purchased. Lemon juice works well in a solution of one part juice to one part water. Neither one will really alter the taste of your dried fruit.

Whichever route you take, you will want to soak your sliced fruit for about five to ten minutes. Then strain out the fruit, and drain well. Do not pat dry or do anything else to remove excess solution. Then load up your dehydrator.

Another way to protect the color of your dried fruit is with sulphur, which is commonly used in commercially produced dried fruit. It is not easy to do at home, and the health concerns of adding sulphur can be an issue. Most home dehydrators prefer to stick to the acid dip method.

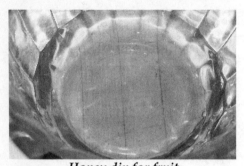

Honey dip for fruit
Photo courtesy of Douglas and Sherri Brown

One more dip option is honey. This is more for taste than anything else, but a quick dip in a dilute honey mixture can add extra sweetness to your final fruit. It is a nice touch for any dried fruit that will be eaten while dry. Stir one cup of liquid honey into 2 cups of hot water. Dip the fruit slices in the mixture for a few moments before loading up the dehydrator.

Assessing dryness

Herbs are done when they crumble, which makes them easy to judge. Fruit is different, and you will not always be looking for the same results. Typically, a

Dried apples and bananas
Photo courtesy of Douglas and Sherri Brown

completely dry piece of fruit will be leathery and pliable rather than dried to a crisp. This is perfectly acceptable and what most people are looking for, especially in fruit you intend to eat while still dry.

Some fruits, such as apples or raspberries, can be dried to a hard texture if the slices are thin enough. They might last longer this way but are not as appetizing to eat dry this way. They work better for rehydrating purposes.

Methods for Drying Fruit

Most methods except for the microwave will work well enough for fruit, though the high moisture content does make some methods better than others.

Sun drying fruit

Drying fruit outdoors in the sun can be difficult because the sugar will attract insects and animal pests. However you set up your drying racks or trays, they must be covered with screen or mesh. Cheesecloth also works well as long as you do not just drape it over your trays of sliced food. It will stick and become permanently attached to your slices of dried fruit.

Fruit contains a lot of moisture, so sun drying can take a long time — often more than two days of exposure. You can take advantage of the full sun because fruits are sturdier than the delicate herbs.

Air drying fruit

Air drying is not generally suitable for fruit because fruit will start to mold before the drying is complete. There is just too much moisture for passive drying like this unless you have thin slices of fruit and a warm area to work in.

Photo courtesy of Douglas and Sherri Brown

Dehydrating fruit

Using a dehydrator is really the best way to dry fruit, particularly if you do not want to wait days to use the sun. Fruit can be sticky, so spraying your dehydrator racks or trays with a nonstick cooking spray can make your life easier later on when it comes time to pry the dry pieces off.

Some fruits can be dried within eight to ten hours, but some should be left overnight or longer. Unless you know your food still requires a full night of drying, you might be better off turning the machine off and then restarting it in the morning when you are around to monitor the dryness.

Oven drying fruit

You will be able to turn your oven up slightly compared to drying herbs. But it still may be too low for some ovens (about 115 F). Like with the dehydrator, drying fruit will stick to your pans. Coat with parchment paper or spray with a non-stick spray before you lay out your sliced fruits.

More moisture will be coming out of fruit than from herbs, so you must leave the door of the oven open while you are drying or the excess water will stay trapped within the oven. This will create a humid environment, and moisture will not come out of the fruit.

Microwaves are not suitable at all for drying fruit. There is just too much water to be removed for a microwave to handle the job.

Storing Dried Fruit

Dried fruit sometimes still can be sticky even after fully dry, so storing in paper is not suitable. Any type of airtight container in glass or plastic will do. Light can discolor

Dried apricots

fruit and turn it dark or brown, so your container should either be opaque or kept in a dark cupboard or cabinet.

When your fruit is fresh out of the dehydrator, let it cool down to room temperature before packing it away in a container.

Because of the natural stickiness of dried fruit, vacuum packing may not be the best approach unless you have dried your fruit to a hard or brittle texture. A vacuum-sealed bag will collapse in on itself, and your fruit is much more likely to stick together. After time in storage, this can lead to a hard-to-manage lump inside the bag.

Specific Instructions for Drying Fruits

The previous chapter on herbs was simpler because all herbs are generally the same size, shape, and thickness (for the most part). Fruit gets more complicated because you are dealing with more variables. The ripeness of your particular batch of fruit and how thinly you cut your slices will both alter the drying time considerably. Instructions here are a good starting point, but always use your own judgment when determining whether your batch is dry.

If you are using a sun- or oven-drying technique with a solid tray or baking sheet, you should turn your fruit pieces over halfway through the estimated time to make sure they are drying evenly. The ventilated trays of a dehydrator do not need this step.

As mentioned in the section above, some fruits should be pretreated before drying. These instructions will be included below as well, as are tips on how to rehydrate your fruit. Most of these are eaten dry, but if you prefer to soften them up, then their texture will be more like cooked fruit. You cannot make dried fruit be truly "fresh" in texture again.

 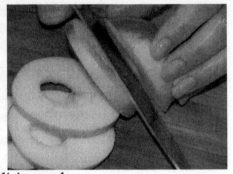

Coring and slicing apples
Photos courtesy of Douglas and Sherri Brown

Apples

Some people peel their apples before drying; some do not. The peel can be a little tough if left on. Once cored, you can cut across into rings or cut lengthwise into slices. Depending on your taste, you can dry apples until they are brittle, but a leathery texture is fine as well.

> *Dehydrator:* Set at 115 F, six to eight hours.
> *Sun drying:* Two to three days
> *Oven:* Set at 115 F, six to eight hours.
> *Treatment:* Will brown, so treat with an acid dip.
> *To rehydrate:* Eat dry or simmer for about half an hour in equal
> parts fruit and water.

Bananas

If you have purchased store-bought banana chips in the past, do not be surprised if the taste and texture of your dried banana slices are different. Most bagged banana chips have been fried rather than dried. They are much crisper and sweeter. To dry bananas, just peel, and slice to about a ¼-inch thickness. Banana is sticky

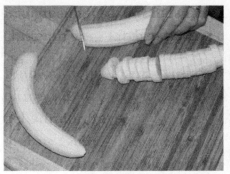

Slicing and placing bananas on the dehydrator tray
Photos courtesy of Douglas and Sherri Brown

and will certainly stick to your pans or trays. To be thoroughly dry, they should be hard.

> *Dehydrator:* Set at 115 F, eight to ten hours.
> *Sun drying:* Two to three days
> *Oven:* Set to 115 F, eight to ten hours.
> *Treatment:* Treat with a dip to prevent browning.
> *To rehydrate:* Dried bananas are eaten dry. They do not refresh
> well.

Oranges

Oranges are not as commonly dried as some other fruits, but it can be done. Because of the membrane between the segments, dried oranges will be tough and are not eaten like other dried fruits. They can be used to flavor drinks or add to brewed teas. Just wash and slice into rounds, with the peels on. Because you are not going to be eating the dried pieces, the added peel gives more flavor. It also helps the slices hold their shape better.

> *Dehydrator:* Set at 130 F, eight to 12 hours or more.
> *Sun drying:* Two days
> *Oven:* Set to 130 F, anywhere from six to ten hours.
> *Treatment:* None needed
> *To rehydrate:* Not usually rehydrated, just used dry

Pineapples

Use either a whole fresh pineapple that has been peeled, cored and sliced, or canned slices. Chunked pineapple might also work, but the pieces might be too thick. Drying pineapple takes much longer than most other fruits, so prepare your timing accordingly.

Dehydrator: Set at 115 F, 24 to 36 hours (continuous time).
Sun drying: Up to five days
Oven: Set to 115 F, 30 to 40 hours.
Treatment: Not necessary
To rehydrate: Eat dry, or simmer 40 minutes with equal parts
fruit and water.

Apricots

Your fruit will need to be sliced open to remove the pits, and you can either chop the fruit or dry the entire halves. The skins can be tough after drying; so, try to peel apricots before you dehydrate them. Submerge whole fruit in boiling water for just a minute, and then cool quickly in ice water. You should be able to pull the skins off with no trouble.

Dehydrator: Set at 115 F, halves — 36 to 40 hours, slices — ten
to 14 hours.
Sun drying: Halves — four days, slices — two days
Oven: Set at 115 F, Halves — 36 hours, slices — 12 hours.
Treatment: Dip treatment is necessary.
To rehydrate: Eat dry or simmered in water for 45 minutes.

Strawberries

Strawberries should have no soft spots when being dried and require little preparation. Just remove the leafy hulls and slice into ¼-inch slices. They dry quickly for fruit, but unlike most other fruits, your slices will be brittle when dry rather than leathery.

Dehydrator: Set at 115 F, ten to 16 hours.

Sun drying: One to two days in direct sun

Oven: Set at 115 F, 18 to 22 hours.

Treatment: Not necessary

To rehydrate: Eat dry, or simmer 1 cup of fruit in 1 cup of water for 30 minutes.

Photos courtesy of Douglas and Sherri Brown

Raspberries

You can use the same techniques and timing for raspberries, blackberries, boysenberries, and loganberries. Wild berries of these types can be dried, but if they are very seedy, they will produce tough fruit after dehydrating. They just need to be washed and can be dried whole. You will want to dry them until they are hard, and you should move them around on their trays during drying.

Dehydrator: Set at 115 F, 24 to 36 hours.

Sun drying. Three to four days in full sunlight

Oven: Set at 115 F, two to three days.

Treatment: No treatment is required

To rehydrate: Simmer 1 cup berries in 1 cup water for 45 minutes to an hour.

Blueberries

The skin on a blueberry needs to be opened up before drying, which can be a little tedious. You either can slice your berries in half or dunk them in boiling water until their skins split naturally. That should only take a few seconds. Just make sure to pat them dry before loading them into the oven or dehydrator. Unlike the raspberries, a thoroughly dry blueberry still will have a little give to it and not be completely brittle.

> *Dehydrator:* Set at 115 F, 12 to 24 hours.
> *Sun drying:* Two to three days
> *Oven:* Set at 115 F, 12 to 24 hours.
> *Treatment:* None
> *To rehydrate:* Eat or cook with dry, or soak for three to four hours in an equal amount of water.

Peaches

You can use the same technique as apricots to remove the skin; just dunk the fruit in boiling water for about a minute and then into ice water. The skin will practically fall off. Also, like apricots, you can dry peaches in halves or slices. But because peaches are larger, trying to dry halves can take a long time. Most people just stick to slices to speed things up a little. These instructions apply to nectarines as well. When completely dried, slices of peach will be quite hard and leathery but not actually brittle.

> *Dehydrator:* Set at 115 F, ten to 12 hours.
> *Sun drying:* Two to three days, in full sun
> *Oven:* Set at 115 F, 12 to 14 hours.
> *Treatment:* Will darken without acid dip
> *To rehydrate:* Eat as is, or simmer in water for about 20 minutes to refresh.

Pears

Some varieties of pear have a distinctive light grittiness to their flesh, which can be magnified if you dry your slices too thinly. For just preserving the fruit, that is fine, but if you want to snack on dried pieces, make sure you do not let them dry hard and brittle. You can leave the skin on if you wish. Make sure your fruit is well ripened before drying.

Dehydrator: Set at 115 F, 12 to 16 hours.
Sun drying: Two to three days in full sun
Oven: Set at 115 F, 14 to 18 hours.
Treatment: Pears need dip treatment.
To rehydrate: Might be too tough for dry eating, rehydrate by simmering for 30 to 45 minutes.

Cherries

Cherries will require a bit more work because they need to be pitted before drying. Once pitted, you should cut each cherry in half so it dries better. Either sweet or tart cherries can be dried the same way. A properly dried cherry will be a lot like a raisin in texture.

Dehydrator: Set at 115 F, 12 to 14 hours.
Sun drying: One to two days in sunlight
Oven: Set to 115 F, 12 to 16 hours.
Treatment: No pretreating is needed.
To rehydrate: Either simmer until soft, or soak 1 cup fruit in 1 cup water overnight.

Kiwi Fruit

You definitely need to peel the fuzzy kiwi before drying. Cut your slices no thicker than ¼ inch, usually cutting across the fruit rather than into wedges. The dark seeds in a kiwi are edible and should pose no problems when drying, so you do not need to worry about removing them. When done, kiwi slices will be leathery.

Dehydrator: Set at 115 F, 12 to 14 hours.

Sun drying: About two days

Oven: Set to 115 F, 16 to 20 hours.

Treatment: Treat to prevent discoloration.

To rehydrate: Eat dry, or simmer in equal parts water for about 40 minutes.

 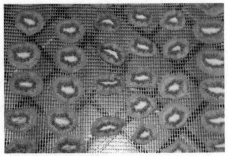

Photos courtesy of Douglas and Sherri Brown

Cantaloupe

Cantaloupe is a dense fruit, but it can be dried, too. Remove the heavy rind, and slice into small pieces (no thicker than ¼ inch). Slices or chunks would be fine. Smaller pieces will dry faster if you do not want to wait quite so long. Dried pieces will be pliable but tough.

Dehydrator: Set at 115 F, 24 to 36 hours (including overnight).

Sun drying: Up to five days

Oven: Set to 115 F, 24 to 30 hours.

Treatment: Not necessary

To rehydrate: Simmer for 20 minutes to half an hour.

Mangoes

For successful drying, get only ripe mangos that are slightly soft to the touch. You must peel them because their skin is not edible even when eat-

en fresh off the fruit. There is a large pit in a mango, so cut slices around that. Mangoes will be very sticky when drying, so treat your pan or trays with a light cooking oil spray.

Dehydrator: Set at 115 F, ten to 12 hours
Sun drying: 24 to 30 hours
Oven: Set at 115 F, 14 to 16 hours.
Treatment: May be necessary, but mango only darkens slightly
    without it.
To rehydrate: One part water and one part fruit, and simmer
    for about half an hour.

Lemons

As with oranges, the segmented form in lemons (any citrus fruit, actually) makes them poor candidates for drying. But a dried slice of lemon can be nice to flavor cold drinks, so there is still a use for it even if it is not a fruit you will likely eat as a dried snack. You can use these instructions to dry limes in the same way. Slice your lemons with the peel on into ¼ inch slices. Remove any seeds before drying if you can. The dried slices should be brittle and hard when done.

Dehydrator: Set at 130 F, eight to 12 hours or more.
Sun drying: Two days
Oven: Set to 130 F, anywhere from six to ten hours.
Treatment: None needed
To rehydrate: Not usually rehydrated, just used dry

Watermelon

Even though it is mostly water inside, watermelon works surprisingly well as a dried fruit. It also dries quicker than you might think. Use a seedless variety if you can, and only dry the pink flesh. Quarter-inch slices will dry the fastest but will be thin when they are done (not much thicker than fruit leather). You can dry ½-inch pieces instead as long as you adjust the timing. Because so much moisture is released, do not use the oven because it does not ventilate well enough. The timing for drying watermelon is difficult to narrow down because the fruit can vary greatly in moisture content. Make sure to keep an eye on your drying fruit.

Dehydrator: Set at 115 F, eight to 14 hours (or longer).
Sun drying: Ten to 16 hours
Oven: Not recommended for oven drying
Treatment: No treatment necessary
To rehydrate: Should be eaten dry only, will not rehydrate well

Plums

A dried plum is more commonly known as a prune. They do not need to be peeled, and you can either dry them in halves or chop them into smaller pieces. Halves will be rubbery, but small pieces will be harder.

Dehydrator: Set at 115 F, halves — 18 to 22 hours, chopped
    pieces — eight to 12 hours.
Sun drying: Halves — three to four days, chopped pieces —
    one to two days
Oven: Set at 115 F, Halves — 24 hours, slices — 18 to 20 hours.
Treatment: Dip treatment is not needed.
To rehydrate: Simmer in water for about half an hour, or soak
    overnight.

Grapes

Considering how easy and inexpensive it is to buy dried grapes (also known as raisins), not many people dry grapes at home. But if you have an abundance of fresh grapes to preserve, drying is a good option because raisins are such a versatile dried fruit. You can dry any sort of grape, green or red. They can be cut in half or dried whole. Whole grapes will need their skins sliced or pricked open so the moisture can get out. You should dry only seedless ones whole. It is usually quickest to cut them in half. A dried grape will be just like a store-bought raisin when done.

Dehydrator: Set at 115 F, 24 to 36 hours.
Sun drying: Three to four days
Oven: Set at 115 F, two to three days.
Treatment: Not needed
To rehydrate: Simmer for half an hour, though many recipes do call for raisins rather than rehydrated grapes.

Cranberries

Drying a cranberry is a lot like drying a blueberry. You will have to open up the skin; so, either score them with a knife, or drop the fruit into boiling water until the skins split open. Dry them well afterward before putting them in the dehydrator or oven.

Finished cranberries will have a raisin-like texture.

Dehydrator: Set at 115 F, 12 to 24 hours.
Sun drying: Two to three days
Oven: Set at 115 F, 12 to 24 hours.
Treatment: Unnecessary
To rehydrate: Soak for two to three hours.

Figs

Slice fresh figs in half and remove the seeds. Like apricots, they typically are dried in halves, but you can dice it up if you prefer smaller pieces. Because they are so fleshy, figs dry better a little warmer than most other fruits, so note the change in temperature. They will be pliable and leathery when completely dried.

Dehydrator: Set at 120 F, ten to 14 hours.
Sun drying: Two days in direct sunlight
Oven: Set at 120 F, 12 to 14 hours.
Treatment: No pretreatment for figs
To rehydrate: You can eat figs dry; otherwise, simmer them in water for about 45 minutes.

Currants

You need to split the skins before drying, which you can do in several ways. You can pierce your currants with a fork before drying or drop them in boiling water for about 30 seconds. Their skins will pop naturally this way, although you will have to drain and thoroughly pat them dry before you load them into the dehydrator. When ready, they will be chewy like a raisin.

Dehydrator: Set at 115 F, 18 to 22 hours.
Sun drying: Two to three days in direct sun
Oven: Set at 115 F, 24 to 30 hours.
Treatment: Just the boiling dip to split the skins
To rehydrate: Currants do not rehydrate well; so, you can just use them as a dry fruit in any recipe you might use raisins.

Persimmons

The persimmon may not be as common a fruit as others here, but it is quite popular in many Asian regions. You will want to choose a firm fruit rather than a soft one for drying, which means you have to have a sweet variety. The astringent types are only sweet once they soften almost to a jelly, and they cannot be dried well. Peel, and slice into ¼-inch slices. A properly dried persimmon will be leathery to the touch.

Dehydrator: Set at 115 F, 18 to 20 hours.
Sun drying: Three to four days
Oven: Set at 115 F, 24 to 30 hours.
Treatment: No pretreatment required
To rehydrate: Once dried, persimmons are usually used that way. Chopped, they can be added to most baked goods.

Quince

Quinces are too sour and astringent to eat unless cooked or extremely ripe. For drying purposes, you should make sure you have a ripe fruit, or your dehydrated fruit will not taste good. You can peel them if you wish, and slice them into ¼-inch pieces.

Dehydrator: Set at 115 F, 12 to 16 hours.
Sun drying: Two to three days in full sun
Oven: Set at 115 F, 14 to 16 hours.
Treatment: Quinces should be dipped to prevent browning.
To rehydrate: Soften up quinces by simmering for half an hour to 45 minutes in equal parts water.

Papaya

Papayas are a little tropical to be found in most gardens, but if you can get fresh ones at the supermarket, you can dry them into tasty fruit snacks. Peel the fruit,  and remove the pit; then slice into ½-inch slices. Dried papaya will be tough but not brittle when done.

Dehydrator: Set at 125 F, 14 to 22 hours.

Sun drying: Two to three days, set in direct sunlight

Oven: Set at 125 F, 18 to 24 hours.

Treatment: Use an acid dip for papaya.

To rehydrate: Eat dry, or simmer in water for about 30 minutes.

Avocado

This is one of the few foods that does not dehydrate well. The avocado has an extremely high fat content, and those oils do not dehydrate away. Even if you were able to get a reasonable level of moisture out, the pieces of fruit would go rancid quickly. A dehydrator is not recommended with avocado.

Dates

Dates generally are found in the stores already dried, but it is possible to dry your own dates if you have access to fresh ones. Even some dried dates can be dried further for longer storage life, as they are probably not completely dry.

For fresh dates, slice open the fruit, and take out the pit. Slice into halves for drying. Dates will be leathery when fully dry.

Dehydrator: Set at 115 F, 14 to 16 hours.

Sun drying: About one day in full sunlight

Oven: Set at 115 F, 18 to 20 hours.

Treatment: You do not need to treat dates.

To rehydrate: Dried dates typically are eaten dry rather than rehydrated.

Grapefruit

Grapefruit is another option for drying citrus fruit, and the tart flavor is a nice change from dried oranges. Slice your fruit into ¼ inch pieces, and remove what seeds you can. When dry, the hard slices can be used in potpourri or to add flavor to lemonade or even plain water.

> *Dehydrator:* Set at 130 F, eight to 12 hours or more.
> *Sun drying:* Two days in full sun
> *Oven:* Set to 130 F, six to ten hours.
> *Treatment:* None is needed.
> *To rehydrate:* Not usually rehydrated, just used dry

Recipes Using Dried Fruit

Although using dried fruits as a snack is common, you can use all kinds of dehydrated fruit in baking and cooking, too. If you are using a standard recipe that calls for fresh fruit, you should rehydrate as per the above instructions *before* using the fruit because the recipe will not have enough liquid otherwise. Or you can use one of these recipes designed specifically for dried fruit.

These are recipes for actual cooking or baking with fruit. *To make mixes for trail mix, refer to Chapter 12 for dry mixes later in the book. Also, Chapter 7 talks about making fruit leather.*

Dried Apple Cobbler

A cobbler is a crustless fruit dish, with a fluffy baked topping over sweet cooked fruit. You can be creative with this one and substitute one cup of peaches, apricots, or pears to change the flavor.

For the fruit:

- 2 cups dried apples
- ¼ cup white sugar

- 1 Tbsp. flour
- 1 cup apple juice, or water

For the topping:

- ¼ cup brown sugar
- ½ cup milk
- ¼ cup vanilla yogurt
- ¼ cup butter
- 1 cup flour
- 1 Tbsp. cinnamon
- ½ tsp. baking powder
- ¼ tsp. baking soda

Before you start, preheat your oven to 375 F.

Combine the first four ingredients for the fruit in an 8-inch baking dish. Bake for about 20 minutes until it begins to bubble.

While that is baking, you can prepare the batter for the topping. Beat sugar, milk, yogurt, and softened butter together in a large mixing bowl. Add in the remaining topping ingredients, and stir until it is all *just* combined (do not overmix).

Pour the batter over the cooked fruit in the baking dish. Put it back in the oven to bake for another half hour until the topping starts to brown on top. Serve your cobbler warm.

Banana Chip Cookies

Both banana chips and chocolate chips give these easy cookies great taste.

- 2 cups flour
- ½ tsp. baking soda
- ½ tsp. baking powder

- ¼ tsp. salt
- ½ cup butter
- 1 cup brown sugar
- 2 eggs
- 2 tsp. vanilla
- 1 cup dried banana chips, chopped
- ⅔ cup chocolate chips

Preheat your oven to 375 F. You will need two baking sheets for this recipe.

In a mixing bowl, stir together the flour, baking soda, baking power, and salt. Set that aside, and beat the butter and sugar together in another bowl until thick. Keep beating, and add the eggs. Mix in the vanilla extract at this point. Then slowly add in the earlier flour mixture, mixing until moist and blended. Fold in banana and chocolate chips

Use a heaping tablespoon of dough to make cookies with at least 2 inches between them (they will spread). Bake for 7 to 8 minutes. They might not seem done, but do not bake them any longer. Let them cool on a rack before eating. You should get about 2 dozen cookies.

Dried Fruit Granola Bars

This is an excellent recipe for using several different types of dried fruit, and you can adjust it to suit your own tastes. Just about any type of chopped dried fruit could be used in place of the ones listed in the recipe.

- 2 cups rolled old-fashioned oats
- 1/3 cup almonds
- 3 Tbsp. sunflower seeds
- 2 Tbsp. flax seeds
- 1 Tbsp. sesame seeds
- 1/4 cup dried cherries
- 1/4 cup dried apricots
- 1/4 cup dried cranberries
- 1/4 cup raisins
- 1/4 cup peanut butter
- 2 Tbsp. brown sugar
- 1/4 cup honey
- 1 tsp. vanilla

Preheat your oven to 350 F, and chop all dried fruits into small pieces. Grease an 8-inch baking pan, and set it aside.

On a cookie or baking sheet, spread out oats, almonds, sunflower seeds, flax seeds, and sesame seeds, and bake for about ten minutes (the oats will start to brown). Pour all your roasted seeds into a mixing bowl. Stir in your dried fruit.

In a small saucepan, heat peanut butter, sugar, honey, and vanilla until it melts and starts to bubble a little bit. Pour the liquid peanut butter mixture over the mix of grains and fruit, and stir through. Spread into the greased baking pan. Make sure it spreads into the corners and is patted down well. Refrigerate until cooled through and firm. Cut into bars.

Spiced Pear Compote

A sweet and spicy way to serve up some dried pears. This would work well with apples, peaches, or apricots, too.

- 2 cups hot water
- 1 cup dried pears
- 3 Tbsp. brown sugar
- 1 tsp. dried lemon zest
- 3 whole cloves
- Cinnamon

Combine all the ingredients together (except for the cinnamon), and simmer together for about half an hour. Serves about four. Top with a sprinkle of ground cinnamon.

Pineapple Muffins

You can still get a moist muffin even when cooking with dried fruit. In this particular recipe, you will need to soften the fruit up a bit before baking instead of just mixing in the dry pieces.

- 1 cup dried pineapple pieces
- 1 ¼ cup boiling water
- 2 ½ cups flour
- ½ cup bran
- 2 tsp. baking powder
- ½ tsp. baking soda
- ¼ tsp. salt
- ½ tsp. nutmeg
- ½ tsp. ginger
- ¾ cup dark brown sugar
- 1 egg
- ¾ cup plain yogurt or sour cream
- ¼ cup butter, melted

First, pour boiling water over the pineapple pieces, and let it sit for half an hour until softened up. While that is soaking, heat up the oven to 375 F.

Add the soaked pineapple to a blender, and purée. Set aside. In another large bowl, sift together flour, bran, baking powder, baking soda, salt, nutmeg, and ginger. Beat the brown sugar, egg, yogurt, and butter into the puréed pineapple until everything is mixed and dissolved.

Then, add the liquid mixture into the bowl with the dry ingredients, and stir a few times so everything mixed and moist. Do not stir more than necessary.

Pour batter into a muffin tray to make 12 muffins. Bake for about 25 minutes until a toothpick comes out clean.

Spicy Mango Salsa

Not all dried fruit recipes have to be baked goods. A mix of dried mango and a few fresh ingredients can make an excellent summer dish or condiment.

- 1 cup dried mango pieces, chopped
- 2 Roma tomatoes, chopped
- ½ small onion, diced
- 1 small avocado, chopped
- Juice from 1 lime
- 1 tsp. jalapeno pepper, minced (more if you like it hot)
- ¼ cup fresh cilantro, minced

Let dried mango pieces soak in water for about 15 minutes, then drain, and combine all the other ingredients together. Let it chill in the refrigerator for half an hour before serving.

Cream and Berry Pie

It is a good idea to soften up the berries first, but they will finish rehydrating during the rest of the cooking process on their own. It is a rich and creamy way to use several kinds of dried berries.

- ½ cup dried strawberries
- ¼ cup dried blueberries
- ¼ cup dried raspberries
- 1 envelope packet of unflavored gelatin
- 2 tsp. vanilla
- 1 ½ cups heavy whipping cream (35%)
- ½ icing sugar
- 1 9-inch piecrust, already baked
- Water

Soak strawberry slices in water for about 15 minutes to start softening them up. Simmer the dried blueberries and raspberries over low heat to do the same. Let all your fruit cool once soft.

In a small mixing bowl, combine the gelatin powder with ¼ cup of water, and let it sit for about five minutes. Pour the gelatin mixture over the strawberries, and stir over low heat until completely dissolved. Let it cool down to room temperature, and then stir in the other berries and the vanilla extract.

Next, whip the cream in a chilled bowl until it starts to develop soft peaks. Then beat in the icing sugar until you get more firm peaks in the cream. Stir the berries gently into the cream; then fill up the pie shell. Refrigerator for an hour if you need to serve it right away, but overnight will be better to let it firm up.

Mediterranean Apricot and Ginger Chicken

This recipe is a little more in-depth than the others, but it is a delicious and unusual way to use dried apricots.

- 2 boneless chicken breast halves
- 1 tsp. cumin
- 3 Tbsp. olive oil
- 2 cloves garlic, minced
- ¾ cup sliced dry apricots
- ¾ cup white wine
- ¼ cup vegetable broth
- 12 pitted green olives

Sprinkle chicken with cumin and fry with olive oil in a skillet until well browned. Remove from heat, and set aside. Cook garlic in the skillet for about 30 seconds; then add the apricots, wine, broth, and olives. Bring to a low boil and simmer until you have a thick sauce. It should take about five minutes. Move the chicken back to the skillet, and cook until the chicken is done and the apricots are tender. Serve right away.

Dried Apple Pie

You should rehydrate the apples a little for this recipe, but they do the rest of their softening while the pie is baking.

- Apple juice
- 4 cups dried apples
- ¼ cup lemon juice
- ¼ cup flour
- 1 cup sugar
- 2 tsp. cinnamon
- ½ tsp. nutmeg
- ¼ tsp. ground cloves

- 3 Tbsp. butter
- Double piecrust

Pour enough warm apple juice over the dried apples to just cover them, and let them sit for half an hour. When they are soft, start your oven preheating to 425 F.

Drain the apples and stir the lemon juice through the fruit. In another small mixing bowl, combine flour, sugar, cinnamon, nutmeg, and cloves. Stir the flour mixture through the apples to cover everything. Pour into your bottom piecrust.

Dot small pats of butter over the apples, and cover with the second crust. Cut a few slits in it, and crimp the edges down. Bake for 15 minutes; then turn the temperature in the oven down to 375 F. Bake for an additional half hour. Serve warm.

Banana Pancakes

These easy pancakes are quick in the mornings, and the added bananas make them healthy and tasty too.

- ½ cup dried banana slices
- 2 cups milk
- 1 ¾ cups flour
- 2 tsp. baking powder
- 2 eggs
- 2 Tbsp. brown sugar (more if you like sweet pancakes)

Simmer banana pieces in milk until they start to soften up, then remove from heat, and let the mixture cool down. Add to a blender canister (do not strain out the milk), and purée until smooth. Add eggs, sugar, and butter until well combined. In a mixing bowl, sift together the flour and baking powder. Mix the banana mixture and the dry ingredients until everything is smooth and moist.

Drop about a quarter cup of batter onto a hot skillet, and cook until you start to see bubbles on the top. Then flip them over, and do the other side until each pancake is nicely browned. Serve with syrup while they are still warm.

Cran-Oat Cookies

These healthful oat cookies could also be made with dried cherries or blueberries for a change of flavor.

- ⅔ cup brown sugar
- ⅔ cup butter, soft
- 2 eggs
- 1 ½ cups rolled oats (not quick oats)
- 1 ½ cups flour
- 1 tsp. baking soda
- 1 cup dried cranberries

Preheat the oven to 375 F.

Beat sugar and butter together with a mixer until they are smoothly mixed and fluffy. Add the eggs, and keep mixing until smooth.

In another bowl, stir together the oats, flour, and baking soda. Then add this mixture to the beaten sugar mixture. Stir until everything is combined and moist. Fold in the dried berries. Drop spoonfuls of batter on a cookie sheet, and bake for about ten minutes. You should get about 24 cookies.

Irish Barm Brack

Barm Brack is a traditional Irish dessert that uses several different types of dried fruit. You will need to start preparing this the night before.

- ½ cup chopped dried apricots
- ½ cup chopped dried peaches
- ½ cup chopped dried cherries or cranberries
- 1 cup brewed black tea
- 1 cup sugar
- 1 egg, light beaten
- 1 Tbsp. orange marmalade
- ½ tsp. cinnamon
- ¼ tsp. allspice
- 1 ¾ cup flour

Stir together all the dried fruit, and soak overnight in tea.

The next day, preheat the oven to 350 F. Then add sugar, marmalade, and beaten egg to the soaked fruit. Stir until sugar is dissolved and everything is mixed. Next, slowly stir in the flour and spices.

Spread the batter into a 9-inch baking pan, and bake for 35 minutes. Serve warm.

Cherry Marmalade

You can really substitute any dried fruit for this marmalade recipe. Apricots, peaches, strawberries, or blueberries will all work nicely.

- 2 cups dried cherries
- 2 cups hot water
- 1 orange, diced up (including peel)

- 1 pkg. of pectin powder
- 3 cups of sugar
- 2 Tbsp. dried lemon peel

Simmer cherries and pieces of orange in water for about half an hour. Take from heat, and stir in pectin, sugar, and lemon peel. Stir well; then bring the mixture back up to a boil and cook for about two minutes. Stir often to keep it from sticking to the bottom.

Pour the fruit mixture into hot pint jars (should make two). You can either let it set up in the fridge if you are going to use it right way, or process the jars in a boiling water canner for ten minutes to seal them up. If you are not familiar with canning, you should omit this step and use the marmalade right away.

Raspberry and Pear Cake Topping

You need your own cake for this (pound cake or angel food cake), and this makes a rich fruity topping. This should make enough topping for about eight slices of cake, depending on how generous you are with each piece.

- ½ cup dried raspberries
- ½ cup dried pears, chopped
- ½ cup water
- ½ cup sherry
- ⅓ cup cream cheese
- ¼ cup whipped cream
- 3 Tbsp. sugar

Mix the dried fruit with water and sherry, and let sit at room temperature for 20 minutes. Start to heat the mixture until it boils, and then drop the heat down to a simmer. Let it cook for another five minutes. The fruit should be soft, and the liquid should be starting to thicken up. Take the pot from the stove, and let it cool completely.

Meanwhile, in a mixing bowl, beat sugar with cream cheese until it is smooth, and then fold in the whipped cream. Mix the cheese mixture in with the fruit mixture, but only stir a few times so that there are clear swirls of cheese within the fruit. Spoon over slices of cake, and serve.

Apricot Citrus Fruit Topping

Here is another topping recipe that can be used over cake or ice cream.

- ½ cup water
- 1 cup orange juice
- 1 ½ cups dried apricots, chopped
- ¾ cup sugar
- 1 Tbsp. lemon juice

Combine water, juice, and fruit in a saucepan. Heat until it reaches a simmer, and then continue to cook for about 20 minutes. Add the sugar and lemon juice, and stir until the sugar is dissolved. Remove from heat, and either serve as a warm or cold topping.

Golden Dried Fruitcake

This is an ideal recipe for using up a mix of dried fruits all at once. You can adjust the specific fruits to suit your taste or availability. There is enough batter to make two loaves of cake.

- 3 eggs
- 1 cup butter, softened
- 1 cup brown sugar
- 2 cups flour
- ½ tsp. baking soda
- 2 cups of dried peaches or apricots (or a mix)
- ½ cup dried cherries
- ½ cup dried pineapple
- 1 cup raisins
- 1 cup chopped or slivered nuts
- 1 tsp. grated lemon peel

Preheat oven to 300 F, and grease two standard-sized loaf pans.

Separate the eggs, and beat the whites until you have soft peaks. In another bowl, beat butter and sugar together until creamy and smooth. Add in the egg yolks, and beat until combined. Fold the whipped eggs into the sugar mixture.

Add 1 ½ cups of flour and baking soda to the mix and stir well. In another bowl, combine the rest of the flour with the dried fruit, nuts, and lemon peel. Stir through, and add that to the main bowl of batter. Pour into your loaf pans, and bake for just over an hour. A toothpick in the middle should pull out clean.

Blueberry Cheesecake Bars

These rich dessert bars taste like they were made with fresh blueberries. You will be surprised at how easy they are to make.

- ½ cup shortening
- ¾ cup sugar
- 3 eggs
- 1 tsp. almond extract
- ⅓ cup milk

- 1 cup flour
- 1 ¼ tsp. baking powder
- 1 cup dried blueberries
- ¾ cup water
- ½ cup icing sugar
- 6 Tbsp. cream cheese, soft
- 1 tsp. almond extract

Preheat oven to 350 F, and grease a 9-inch baking pan.

First, you mix the water and blueberries and leave them to soak for about an hour.

Next, you need to make the crust for the bars. Mix the shortening, sugar, one of the eggs, milk, and first measure of almond extract into a cream. Then add the flour and baking powder, and stir until everything is moist and combined. Spread the mixture over the bottom of your baking pan, flattening it out to be even.

Spread your softened berries over the crust. Then, in another bowl, beat the last two eggs with the cream cheese and icing sugar. Fold in the almond extract, and spread the creamed mixture over the berries. Bake for an hour, and then let it cool in the pan before you start cutting the bars.

Raisin Sugar Cookies

Though raisins are the most common dried fruit around and recipes are not hard to find, here is one for an easy cookie. You will get about three dozen cookies from each batch.

- ½ cup raisins
- ½ cup water
- ½ tsp. vanilla
- ¼ cup shortening
- ¼ cup butter
- ¾ cup white sugar
- 1 egg
- 1 ¾ cups flour
- ½ tsp. baking soda
- 1 tsp. vanilla

Combine the raisins and water in a saucepan, and stir in first measure of vanilla. Bring it to a boil, and then remove the pot from the heat. Set aside for the moment, and start your oven heating to 350 F.

Mix the shortening, butter, and sugar together until fluffy. Whisk in the egg and the second measure of vanilla. In another bowl, mix the flour with baking soda, and then slowly mix into the creamed sugar mixture. Drain any excess water from the raisins, and then add them in as well.

Roll the soft dough into small balls, and set them out on the cookie sheet about two inches apart. They will spread; so do not crowd them. Bake for eight to ten minutes, and let them cool on a wire rack.

Strawberry Loaf

It is a bit of a cross between a cake and bread. This sweet loaf can be eaten at breakfast or served as a quick casual dessert.

- 1 cup dried strawberries
- 1 cup water
- 1 ½ cups flour

- 1 cup brown sugar
- 2 tsp. cinnamon
- ½ tsp. salt
- ½ tsp. baking soda
- ½ cup vegetable oil
- 2 eggs, lightly beaten
- ½ cup chopped nuts of your liking

Combine dried berries and water, and let soak for about half an hour to an hour. Strain out any extra liquid, and set aside. Then start preheating the oven to 350 F.

In a larger mixing bowl, stir together flour, sugar, cinnamon, salt, and baking soda. Stir the oil and eggs into the strawberries, and then pour into the dry ingredients while you stir. Mix until just moistened (do not overmix), and then fold in the chopped nuts. Pour the batter into a loaf pan, and bake for 50 minutes.

Sweet Apple Squares

These sweet squares are soft like cake but have a crisper crumble topping.

- 1 cup dried apple pieces
- 1 cup water
- 1 cup flour
- 1 tsp. baking powder
- ¼ tsp. cinnamon
- ¼ cup melted butter
- ½ cup brown sugar
- ½ cup white sugar
- 1 egg
- 1 tsp. vanilla
- ½ chopped walnuts or pecans

Before you begin, soak the apple pieces in 1 cup of water for about half an hour. They do not need to be completely rehydrated, just starting to soften up.

When that is done, preheat the oven to 350 F.

In a mixing bowl, sift the flour and baking powder together along with the cinnamon. Set this aside for now. Then in another bowl, mix butter, brown sugar, and white sugar together until the mixture is smooth, and then mix in the egg and vanilla. Slowly add the flour mixture to the butter and sugar mixture until everything is moist, but do not stir more than needed. Fold in the nuts and apples.

Spread the batter into a 9 x 9-inch pan, and bake for 30 to 35 minutes. The tops should be firm when finished. Let them cool in the pan before you slice into squares.

Baked Pears with Currants

Unfortunately, you cannot make this with dried pears, but it is a fine recipe to use dried currants you have on hand. The recipe makes ten pears, so it is suitable for those occasions where you need to serve a crowd.

- 10 firm pears
- ⅔ cup white sugar
- ⅔ cup brown sugar
- 2 tsp. cinnamon
- 1 cup dried currants
- ¾ cup water

Use an apple corer to take the core out of the pear, but leave the pear otherwise intact. If it is uneven on the bottom, slice a little off so it stands upright on its own. Start your oven heating to 350

F at this point. Set up your hollow pears (standing up) in a glass baking dish.

In a small bowl, stir both types of sugar, cinnamon, and the currants. Pour about half of this mixture into the pear holes. Add water to the remaining currant mix, and pour over the pears. Bake until the pears are soft. If the syrup gets too thick in the meantime, add a little water while it bakes. Spoon some of the syrup over the pears while it bakes as well. It should take about 45 minutes. Serve while still warm.

Fig and Cranberry Nut Stuffing

This may not be a typical everyday kind of recipe, but it is a nice gourmet touch to serve with a turkey or any meal you like.

- 1 loaf of bread (any style, your preference)
- ¾ cup dried cranberries
- 1 cup apple juice
- 1 onion, diced
- 1 cup dried figs, diced
- 1 cup walnuts
- 2 tsp. dried sage
- ¼ cup butter, melted
- ⅔ cup vegetable stock

Preheat oven to 375 F (or whatever temperature you need for your turkey), and cut bread into small cubes. You should have about 6 cups of bread for this recipe to be its best.

In a small saucepan, heat dried cranberries in ¾ cup of apple juice until they are soft. Drain off the extra juice, and then stir the berries into the bowl of bread cubes. Add onion, figs, walnuts, and sage. Back in the saucepan, heat up the last ¼ cup of apple juice, butter, and vegetable stock. Toss the liquid with the bread mixture until everything is slightly moist.

Stuff your turkey or whatever you are stuffing, or pour the mixture out into a casserole dish, and bake on its own for 50 minutes at 375 F.

Chocolate and Prune Brownies

This is not your typical fruit recipe, but it really is an excellent way of using dried plums and making some healthy brownies. With less butter and egg, the prunes keep these treats low fat.

- ¼ cup dried plums, chopped
- ¼ cup water
- 4 oz. semi-sweet chocolate pieces (chips would work)
- 2 Tbsp. butter
- 1 cup sugar
- 1 egg
- 1 egg white
- 2 tsp. vanilla
- ½ tsp. salt
- ¾ cup flour
- ⅓ cup cocoa powder

Before you begin, soak your dried plums (prunes) in water until they are soft. Drop them into the blender and process until pureed.

Preheat your oven to 350 F, and grease an 8-inch baking pan.

Melt chocolate by your preferred method, whether in a double boiler over water or in the microwave. Whisk melted chocolate into sugar, egg and egg white, pureed prunes, vanilla, and salt. Keep whisking until you have a smooth mixture.

In another bowl, stir flour and cocoa powder together. Then add the dry mixture to the liquid chocolate mix, and stir until just combined. Pour batter into the pan, and bake for about half an hour. An inserted toothpick should come out clean.

Mango Squares

These sweet squares are a great dessert and a nice change from the more typical fruits we usually have around the house.

For the crust:

- 1 cup flour
- ¼ cup icing sugar
- ½ cup butter

For the filling:

- 1 cup dried mango pieces, chopped
- 1 cup brown sugar
- ⅓ cup flour
- 2 eggs, lightly beaten
- ½ tsp. baking powder
- ¼ tsp. lemon extract

Preheat your oven to 350 F, and then start to simmer the dried mango pieces in just enough water to cover. They will take about 15 minutes to soften up. Meanwhile, you can start the crust.

In a mixing bowl, mix the first measure of flour with icing sugar. Once they are mixed, cut in the butter until you have a mix of coarse crumbs. Spoon this into a greased 9 x 9-inch baking pan. Press down and into the corners to make a firm crust. Bake for about ten minutes until it starts to brown.

For the filling, stir together the softened mango along with the remaining ingredients in another bowl. Mix until well blended.

Pour out over the baked crust. Spread it to cover evenly. Cover the pan, and bake for 20 minutes until the filling firms up. Let it cool before cutting into squares or bars.

Blueberry and Lemon Scones

These baked treats are not that sweet, and they are nice as a dessert or just to go with a cup of coffee.

- 3 cups flour
- 4 ¼ tsp. baking powder
- 1 tsp. salt
- ½ cup sugar
- ¾ cup butter, cut up
- 1 ½ cups dried blueberries
- 1 cup milk
- 3 Tbsp. grated dry lemon peel

Start your oven heating to 425 F.

Whisk flour and sugar together, and then cut in the butter until you have coarse crumbs. Stir in blueberries. Add milk and lemon peel, and stir until you have firm dough. Turn out onto a floured surface, and give it a few kneads. Split in half, and form each piece into a thick disk. Slice each into six wedges.

Place pieces on a greased baking sheet. Bake for about 20 minutes or until a toothpick comes out clean.

Growing Your Own Fruit

Fruit is easy to grow on your own, although some might not be that suitable for small spaces. In general, fruits are perennials, which mean your plants will continue to grow and produce fruit for years after you initially plant them. It also can mean that it can take a few years to grow large enough to begin giving you a harvest, so patience will be required.

This goes for trees and some bush fruit, such as blueberries. Raspberries and grapes may take a year or two to get established as well. For a quicker fruit harvest, cantaloupe, watermelon, and strawberries will all produce fruit in their first year. Cranberries can give fruit in their first year, but they are finicky when it comes to their soil, and home gardeners do not commonly grow them.

Because it can last several years, make sure you plant your fruit garden in a location where it will not be disturbed. Sunny and fertile locations with good drainage are best. Plan to add a dose of compost or aged manure each year (or more frequently) to keep the soil filled with nutrients.

Some fruit, such as raspberries, grapes, and possibly cantaloupes, should have some kind of support in place to keep the branches and vines up off the ground. There is nothing wrong with letting them grow naturally, but you will get a better fruit harvest with a few stakes, string, or a trellis. Fruit trees are self-sufficient but can require some pruning to keep the trees small and productive. Trimming back dead growth is a good practice even with smaller bushes such as blueberries and raspberries.

You also should know that some fruits, particularly the trees, would require two or more plants to get proper fertilization. Look for trees that are identified as being "self-fertile" if you only have room or need for one. A tree that requires a "mate" will not bear any fruit if planted alone.

Check your local growing zone (**www.usna.usda.gov/Hardzone/ ushzmap.html**) on the next page to see what fruit plants can survive the winters in your area. Do not assume a fruit is too exotic or tropical for your backyard. Many fruit trees and plants have varieties that can survive in colder weather than you might expect.

For the novice gardener, look into starting strawberries first. They can be grown in a small area (even a container) and require little work to get your first berries. Cantaloupes and watermelon are two other good choices to start with because they are annuals. You will just need a little more room because they do spread out unless you use supports. Even someone new at gardening can do well with trees, although they represent a larger cash and time investment and can produce many fruit.

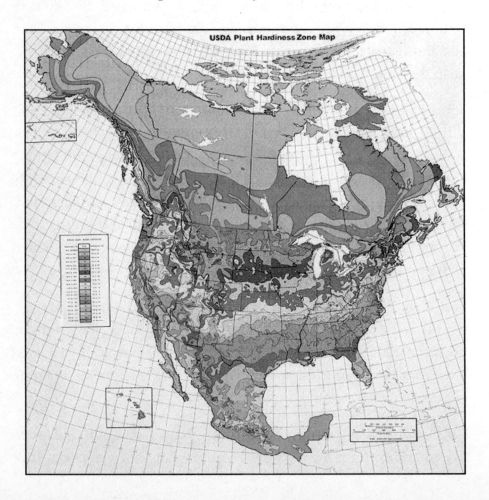

Chapter 6

DRYING VEGETABLES

D ried vegetables are great for preservation and storage, but they are not used often in their dry form like fruit is. Rehydrating them will be more important. Nearly any vegetable can be dried, although some can take a long time.

Preparing Vegetables to Be Dried

There may be a little more prep time required with drying vegetables, although it is still pretty minimal compared to other preservation methods.

Harvesting or buying vegetables for drying

If you intend to preserve most of your garden harvest by drying, it is a good idea to plant accordingly. To maximize your time and effort, you will want enough vegetables at one time to fill up the dehydrator rather than just a handful or so at a time. So, plant your garden with that in mind. Some varieties of green beans, for example, will flower and produce beans all through the summer (usually the vining or pole beans). But for a single, large harvest, bush beans are more likely to flower all at once and then produce their beans.

Even if you do not have your own vegetable garden, you can find plenty of fresh vegetables for your dehydrator. Your local farmers market is usually the best place to find in-season vegetables at the lowest prices. After that, your regular supermarket is ideal for getting lots of produce for drying. Again, stick with whatever is currently in season to get the best buys.

As vegetables are losing some of their freshness, many grocery stores will reduce the prices. As long as you know you will have time to prepare and dehydrate them properly right away, you can use this produce for more savings. Fresh is always better, but you can save some money if you have older produce available on occasion.

Another option is to buy frozen or even canned vegetables for drying. It might not seem like a sensible approach to use food that is already in a preserved state, but there are some good reasons for this approach. Because dried foods take up so little space, you can store more compared to a can that is holding a large volume of water. Frozen vegetables also can be dried if you prefer to not have them taking up space in the freezer.

Cleaning and preparing vegetables

Most vegetables will need to be washed before you do any dehydrating, and many will need to be peeled, cored, and/or seeded. As with fruit, most slices should be about ¼ of an inch thick, but dense vegetables might require thinner pieces to dry adequately. *Specifics are provided in the instructions later in this chapter.*

A handy way to cut vegetables for drying is with a mandolin. Not to be confused with a musical instrument, a mandolin is also a

Mandolin

small slicing gadget that will make your vegetable slicing go much quicker. It consists of a small board with a blade mounted in the middle, and you run your vegetable back and forth to slice. By adjusting the posi tion of the blade, you can control the thickness of your slices. It does not work as well for soft fruits, but it can be a great timesaver when slicing up vegetables for drying. It also means more consistency, which will lead to better dehydrating results.

Go through your vegetables and cut out any bruised, discolored, or damaged spots.

Additional vegetable preparations

There may be one more step before you start with your dehydrating, and that is blanching. It is not usually a necessary step with fruit, but it can be important with vegetables. Blanching just means to dunk your sliced vegetables in boiling water for a few minutes, long enough to stop the enzyme action that will lead to deterioration of the food in storage. Drying itself does not do this. A blanch usually takes about two to three minutes on average once you have the water to the boiling point. If you intend to use your dried food quickly, you can probably skip this step. For longer-term storage purposes, it is worth the time and effort to prepare properly.

Asparagus in ice water after being blanched.

Get a large pot of water boiling, and submerge your cut vegetables for a few minutes. *Specific timing is provided later in this chapter for each type of vegetable.* Strain, and then dunk again in ice cold water to stop the cooking action. You do not want to actually cook your food, just destroy the enzymes inside. Pat well to dry everything off, and then start up your dehydrator.

Vegetables usually do not discolor with exposure to air, so there is no need for any dip treatments as when drying fruit.

Assessing dryness

Knowing when vegetables are dry enough is much like dehydrating fruit. Some types need to be dried to crispness and some will stay leathery. Knowing what to expect can help you from accidentally overdrying your foods. Each set of instructions given later in this chapter for drying specific vegetables will indicate what you need to look for in your finished product.

The description of "leathery" is common with dehydration, and it means that the item will be tough, not sticky, and will be pliable when bent.

Methods for Drying Vegetables

Though most vegetables are denser than fruits, they also contain less moisture, so they are not that much more difficult to dry.

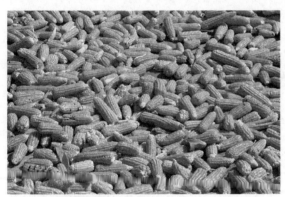

Some will take a few days, and some can be thoroughly dried in just one afternoon.

Sun drying vegetables

Corn laid out to dry in the sun

Drying vegetables outdoors is not as risky as fruit because they are not as appealing to insects and pests. Vegetables are not as sweet and juicy. You still may want to cover your drying food with a mesh cover, just in case. Squirrels and birds might still take off with your vegetables if they are left exposed.

In most cases, vegetables will need to be dried for more than one day. Even so, you should not leave your racks or trays outside overnight. Moisture will settle back on your foods due to the drop in temperature, and most of your drying will be undone.

Air drying vegetables

Air drying can work, but it is not a recommended way to dehydrate vegetables unless you have a warm area with constantly moving air. If you have a wood stove going in your home, that can create a good area for food drying during the fall harvest period.

This was how people dried vegetables a few generations ago, so it definitely does work if you have the right conditions. Keep a close eye on your drying food so nothing starts to spoil. Using air to dry like this will take several days, no matter what type of vegetable you are drying.

It would be a better scenario if you put your food outside in the sun or used either an actual dehydrator or the oven.

Dehydrating vegetables

If you have a dehydrator with a temperature control, vegetables do dry better at 120 F. The timings provided in this section are based on this temperature, so you might have to leave them in for longer if you cannot reach 120 F degrees with your model of dehydrator. You can also slice your veggies thinner to speed up the process.

Because they are not as aromatic as herbs or even fruit, you can mix your vegetables in your dehydrator (or oven) because they generally do not take on one another's flavors. Onions, peppers, and garlic are a few exceptions that should be dried on their own.

Oven drying vegetables

You will be able raise the temperature of your oven to 120 F for nearly all vegetables, which may work better than drying fruit depending on your oven's capabilities. Because vegetables are dense (compared to fruit), stir them up and rotate your trays during drying. This is not as necessary with a dehydrator because of the fan and constant air movement.

Veggies are not generally sticky, so spraying your pans or trays should not be required.

Storing Dried Vegetables

One thing to keep in mind when planning your dried vegetable storage is even just one moist piece can develop mold, which will then spread to the entire container of food. Technically, this can be a problem with all types of dried food, but vegetables tend to be the most problematic because their dense structure can make it hard to get the last bits of moisture out of each piece.

The best way to avoid this is to always make sure to dry all your vegetables to completion. Unfortunately, no one is perfect, and sometimes this does not happen. To prevent the ruin of a huge batch of food, try to store your dried vegetables in small containers. That way, if one gets mold or mildew, it will only spoil one small bunch.

Heavy-duty zip-close bags can work well, even within a larger container to help keep your dried vegetables separated.

Specific Instructions for Drying Vegetables

Carrots

Because they are so dense, cut your carrots thinner than usual, closer to $1/8$ of an inch. This is when a mandolin or automatic slicer would come in handy. You might want to peel  off the outer layer with larger or older carrots, but it is not necessary. If you are not peeling them, scrub the outside well. Once dried, your carrot slices should be tough but pliable.

> *Dehydrator:* Set at 120 F, 12 to 18 hours.
> *Sun drying:* Two to three days in direct sun
> *Oven:* Set to 120 F, 18 to 20 hours.
> *Treatment:* Blanch for two to three minutes.
> *To rehydrate:* 1 cup of water and 1 cup dried carrots, simmered
> for half hour to an hour

Cabbage

Cabbage dries best when shredded, and you should remove the tougher outside leaves before you begin. You can use a mandolin or just slice up chunks of cabbage into fine pieces. When done, the pieces should be crisp.

> *Dehydrator:* Set at 120 F, 12 to 14 hours.
> *Sun drying:* Two to three days in sunlight
> *Oven:* Set at 120 F, 18 to 20 hours.

Treatment: Blanch for one to two minutes.

To rehydrate: 1 cup of water and 1 cup dried cabbage shreds, simmer for 40 minutes.

Corn

You can dry corn that has been purchased in kernel form (either frozen or canned) or fresh kernels you have stripped off the cob. If you are going to try frozen kernels, you can just load up your trays with them still frozen. They thaw so quickly that it really does not affect your drying times. Dried corn will be hard in texture. If you have a grain grinder, you can make your own cornmeal or corn flour with the dried kernels.

Dehydrator: Set at 120 F, eight to 12 hours.

Sun drying: One to two days

Oven: Set at 120 F, 12 to 14 hours.

Treatment: Blanch for two to three minutes.

Rehydrate: Simmer 2 cups water to 1 cup corn for about an hour.

Tomatoes (Ripe)

When drying ripe tomatoes, you will have to remove the skins first. Heat them quickly in boiling water for one minute, and then cool quickly in ice water for another minute. The skins will slip off easily. Remove the  seeds and the cores. Either slice tomatoes or dry them in small, diced chunks. The pieces will be brittle when done.

Dehydrator: Set at 120 F, 14 to 16 hours.

Sun drying: One to two days in direct sun

Oven: Set at 120 F, 16 to 20 hours.

Treatment: None needed

Rehydrate: Soak in warm water for one hour.

Tomatoes (Green)

You also can dry green (unripe) tomatoes, which work particularly well for the traditional fried green tomato recipes. Choose firm but unripened fruit for this, and you do not need to skin them. Dry either sliced or diced. Like ripe tomatoes, they will be crisp when dried enough.

Dehydrator: Set at 120 F, 12 to 16 hours.

Sun drying: Two to three days

Oven: Set at 120 F, 18 to 20 hours.

Treatment: None needed

Rehydrate: Soak for about half an hour until soft enough to use. Because green tomatoes are intended to be firm in most recipes, do not let them over-hydrate.

Green Beans

When picking your own green beans, they need to be young enough that the seeds have not started to thicken inside the long pods. You can dry beans whole or chopped into smaller pieces. Chopped ones will dry in a more reasonable amount of time. When they are completely dry, the pieces will be a little pliable rather than brittle.

Dehydrator: Set at 120 F, ten to 12 hours.

Sun drying: Two to three days in direct hot sun

Oven: Set at 120 F, 14 to 18 hours.

Treatment: Blanch for two to three minutes.

To rehydrate: Simmer 1 cup of beans in 2 cups of water for 45 minutes.

Dry Beans

These are a whole group of beans that you normally would purchase dry. This would include navy beans, kidney beans, black-eyed peas, lentils, and lima beans. You seldom buy these beans while fresh, so you would likely only be drying them if you have a harvest in your own garden. The best way to do this is to first let them dry on the vine. Let your plants die back and wait until the beans are already very dry before you even pick them. After dehydrating, these beans should crack when struck with a hammer.

Dehydrator: Set at 120 F, six to eight hours.
Sun drying: One day in full sun
Oven: Set at 120 F, eight to 12 hours.
Treatment: None is necessary, other than vine drying

To rehydrate: Beans like these take longer to rehydrate than most other vegetables; so, do not plan to make them in a quick moment. Soak your beans for at least four hours, and drain the water off. Start cooking them in fresh water, and simmer until they are soft. They cook like any dry bean you have purchased from the store.

Peas

If you are harvesting peas, pick them when they have filled out their pods but before they begin to dry on the vine. Once they dry naturally still on the plant, they will lose most of their flavor.

Shell them out of their pods, and blanch before drying. You also can dehydrate frozen peas if you prefer not to store them in the freezer. Blanching is not necessary if you use frozen peas. They will be hard when dry, with no give or flexibility to them. Do not expect them to end up soft like a raisin.

Dehydrator: Set at 120 F, 12 to 18 hours.
Sun drying: One to two days
Oven: Set at 120 F, 14 to 20 hours.
Treatment: Blanch for about two minutes.
To rehydrate: Add 1 cup of peas to 2 cups of water, and cook until soft (45 minutes).

Potatoes

Potatoes will mold with the slightest amount of moisture, so if you are going to store them, you have to make sure they are completely dry. When drying in slices, they should be thinner than the typical ¼ inch in order to dehydrate properly. Closer to ⅛ inch would be better. You also could dice them, but if the pieces are more than ⅛ inch thick, it will not really speed things up. Peel potatoes before slicing them. When fully dry, they will be tough and brittle.

Dehydrator: Set at 120 F, 14 to 20 hours.
Sun drying: Three days in direct sunlight
Oven: Set at 120 F, 18 to 22 hours.
Treatment: Blanch for six minutes, draining well after.
To rehydrate: With 1 cup of water to 1 cup of potato slices, cook for 50 minutes to an hour.

Sweet Peppers

These instructions are for the large blocky bell peppers, not slim hot or chili peppers. To prepare for drying, remove the core, seeds, and all pieces of white membrane inside. This will add bitterness to your dried peppers if you leave it. Slice the flesh into thin slices, or dry as diced. The final product will be stiff and leathery.

Dehydrator: Set at 120 F, eight to 12 hours.

Sun drying: One to two days in sunlight

Oven: Set at 120 F, 16 to 20 hours.

Treatment: You do not need to blanch peppers for dehydrating.

To rehydrate: You can use small dry pieces as an herb for salads or soups, but you also can rehydrate in about 45 minutes of simmering.

Chili Peppers

Because they are smaller and less fleshy, chili peppers have a different drying time than the previously mentioned sweet bell peppers. You can chop your peppers into pieces or dry them whole (the instructions are for chopped). Because they are used more like a spice than a vegetable, you usually do not refresh them for use. Just add a few dry pieces to whatever you are cooking for the added heat. Chili peppers will be brittle when completely dry. Do not dry with other vegetables, or everything will taste like hot chili.

Dehydrator: Set at 120 F, ten to 16 hours.

Sun drying: One to two days

Oven: Set at 120 F, 18 to 24 hours.

Treatment: No need to pretreat

To rehydrate: Generally not rehydrated, but you can simmer or soak to soften.

Onions

This is another vegetable that should not be mixed with others in a dehydrator, but outdoor drying would be fine to dissipate the flavor and odor. Drying onions is not that com-

mon because dried onion flakes are popular as a spice and can be purchased inexpensively. You can dry either as thin slices or diced. Either way, your onion will be hard when dried.

Dehydrator: Set at 120 F, 12 to 20 hours.

Sun drying: Two to three days

Oven: Set at 120 F, 24 to 30 hours.

Treatment: Do not need to blanch or treat

To rehydrate: Cook dried, or refresh in warm water — soak for about 15 minutes.

Radishes

The peppery taste of radish becomes magnified when you dry it, so use sparingly as a crispy flavoring; otherwise, rehydrate. The thick pieces should be sliced thin, about 1/8 inch. Make sure they are well washed. When finished, your dried radish will be crisp and hard.

Dehydrator: Set at 120 F, eight to ten hours.

Sun drying: One to two days

Oven: Set at 120 F, ten to 12 hours.

Treatment: Radishes should not be blanched or otherwise treated.

To rehydrate: Eat dry, or simmer in water for about 20 minutes.

Spinach

It might not seem like a good candidate for dehydration, but drying spinach does work well. You should chop up the leaves after a good washing and just dry in pieces. You can leave the pieces intact for later rehydration or crumble up the pieces to use almost like an herb. A little dried spinach, even in powdered form, can add a lot of nutrition to existing recipes.

Dehydrator: Set at 120 F, eight to ten hours.

Sun drying: 20 to 26 hours

Oven: Set at 120 F, ten to 12 hours.

Treatment: None is necessary for spinach.

To rehydrate: Either use dried, or simmer in water for about 10 to 15 minutes.

Zucchini

Considering how prolific zucchini can be, many home gardeners are desperate for a way to preserve their huge harvests. If you are going to dry your zucchini (also known as summer squash), you should pick them before the seeds start to develop inside. They can be rehydrated, but many people enjoy  the crisp slices while still dry. Wash and slice to ⅛ of an inch. Peeling is not necessary; so, it is up to you.

Dehydrator: Set at 120 F, six to eight hours.

Sun drying: Eight to ten hours in full sun

Oven: Set at 120 F, six to eight hours.

Treatment: Nothing necessary

To rehydrate: Simmer in equal parts dried zucchini and water for half an hour to 45 minutes.

Winter Squash

Winter squash refers to the various types of squash that have a tough outer rind, which makes them different from zucchini. Acorn and butternut are the two most common, but this also includes Hubbard squash, delecta, and even spaghetti squash. They will all dry the same way. Some people cook squash before drying it, but you can dry the flesh when raw, which saves you the extra time. Cut the flesh away from the rind, and remove all the seeds. Cut into slices no thicker than ¼ inch.

Dehydrator: Set at 120 F, 12 to 14 hours.

Sun drying: Two days in direct sunlight

Oven: Set at 120 F, 16 to 20 hours.

Treatment: Do a boiling water blanch for three minutes.

To rehydrate: With equal parts squash and water, simmer over low heat for 30 to 40 minutes.

Pumpkin

Pumpkin will need to be opened up and all the seeds removed. If you wish, you can save the seeds for their own drying. Then, the thick orange flesh must be sliced out. You can dry it in either thin slices or small cubes, whichever you prefer. When fully dry, pieces of pumpkin will be leathery with no moisture in the middle of each piece.

Dehydrator: Set at 120 F, 16 to 18 hours.

Sun drying: Two to three days in the full sun

Oven: Set at 120 F, 18 to 20 hours.

Treatment: Blanch in boiling water for two minutes; then drain.

To rehydrate: Simmer pumpkin pieces in equal parts pumpkin and water for about 45 minutes.

Broccoli

You can use garden-grown or store-bought broccoli heads, as long as they have not started to open up or turn yellow. They still should be dark green. Both the stalks and florets can be dried though most people prefer to cook with just the floret portions. Cut the heavier stalks away, and chop the florets into small pieces no longer than a half inch. Florets will be crisp when ready, but any stalk pieces will be tough.

Dehydrator: Set at 120 F, ten to 16 hours.

Sun drying: One or two days in direct sun or light shade

Oven: Set at 120 F, 14 to 18 hours.

Treatment: Blanch for two to three minutes.

To rehydrate: Simmer 1 cup of broccoli pieces in 1 ¼ cup water for about half an hour.

Cauliflower

Cauliflower does take a while to dry because it is such a dense vegetable. Cut apart small floret pieces, and remove leaves and heavy stalk pieces. Each floret should be sliced in half so its central stalk is sliced open and exposed to the warm air.

Dehydrator: Set at 120 F, 12 to 16 hours.

Sun drying: Two to three days in direct sunlight

Oven: Set at 120 F, 20 to 32 hours.

Treatment: Short blanch in boiling water for one minute

To rehydrate: Simmer in water for half an hour to 45 minutes until soft.

Rhubarb

Granted, the sour taste of rhubarb usually means it is cooked in sweet dishes, so you may not think of it as a vegetable. But the red stalks are considered a vegetable. Only the stalks can be eaten, so make sure you discard every single leaf (they are actually toxic). For drying, cut stalks into 1-inch pieces, and when done, they will be tough but not crisp. You can use the dried pieces as a tart flavoring with other fruit or rehydrate to use as cooked rhubarb (for instance, in pies or cakes).

Dehydrator: Set at 120 F, 12 to 16 hours.
Sun drying: Two days in full sunlight
Oven: Set at 120 F, 14 to 18 hours.
Treatment: No need to blanch, but a three-minute boil will make your rhubarb less sour.
To rehydrate: Small pieces can be used dry, otherwise simmer in water for about half an hour.

Cucumber

Cucumber might not seem like a good candidate for dehydrating, but it really does work well. A common use is to eat dry slices with dip, almost like a potato chip. You just have to choose slimmer cucumbers that have as few seeds as possible. English cucumbers are good for this. Peel your cucumbers, and slice in to 1/8-inch slices for drying. When they are done drying, they will be brittle.

Dehydrator: Set at 120 F, eight to ten hours.
Sun drying: Two days in direct sunlight
Oven: Set at 120 F, 12 to 14 hours.

Treatment: You do not need to blanch.

To rehydrate: Generally used dry because they will be mushy if you rehydrate them.

Eggplant

When buying or harvesting eggplant, choose one with shiny purple skin that is firm to the touch. Soft eggplant will not dry as well. Peel and slice into ¼-inch slices. You can dry the whole slices, or cut them up further into small cubes. Eggplant has a leather consistency when fully dry.

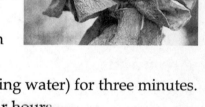

> *Dehydrator:* Set to 120 F, 18 to 20 hours.
>
> *Sun drying:* Three days in full sun
>
> *Oven:* Set to 120 F, 20 to 28 hours.
>
> *Treatment:* Steam blanch (not boiling water) for three minutes.
>
> *To rehydrate:* Soak for three to four hours.

Turnip

When growing your own turnips, you will want to pick them after you have had the first hard frost of the winter. The flavor is much better once they have had that freezing treatment, though you will not be able to take advantage of this if you are buying turnips at the store. Cut the tops off and peel off the outer skin. Slice or cube into pieces about ¼ of an inch in thickness. When your turnip is dry enough, it will be tough and hard.

> *Dehydrator:* Set at 120 F, 14 to 20 hours.
>
> *Sun drying:* Two to three days in direct sunlight
>
> *Oven:* Set at 120 F, 18 to 22 hours.

Treatment: Blanch in boiling water for three minutes.

To rehydrate: Simmer in water for about 45 minutes, with about one part turnip to one part water.

Okra

Whether from the store or the garden, try to select bright green pods that are no longer than 4 inches. Slice them up into ¼-inch pieces for drying. They are a simple vegetable to prepare for dehydrating.

Dehydrator: Set at 120 F, eight to 14 hours.

Sun drying: One or two days in full sun

Oven: Set at 120 F, ten to 16 hours.

Treatment: You will not need to blanch okra before drying.

To rehydrate: In about 2 cups of water to 1 cup of okra, simmer for half an hour to 40 minutes.

Asparagus

Because asparagus is only harvested in the spring, it can be extra helpful to be able to preserve it once it is out of season. Cut fresh spears into ½-inch pieces, and discard any woody ends.

Dehydrator: Set at 120 F, four to eight hours.

Sun drying: One to two days in full sun

Oven: Set at 120 F, 8 to 12 hours.

Treatment: Blanch in boiling water for three minutes.

To rehydrate: Simmer in equal parts water for about 45 minutes.

Kale

These instructions also apply for spinach, collards, or Swiss chard. Use only fresh green leaves, and cut out any limp or browning pieces. If you are going to make a powder, you can chop the pieces up before drying, although they do crumble eas-ily if you choose to just dry the whole leaves first. Kale leaves will hold their shape best when dry and even can be used as a chip with dip. If you leave the leaves relatively whole while drying, you can rehydrate them to use as a cooked vegetable more easily.

Dehydrator: Set at 120 F, ten to 14 hours.
Sun drying: One to two days in the full sun
Oven: Set at 120 F, 16 to 20 hours.
Treatment: Blanch for one minute (no longer).
To rehydrate: Powder can be added as is, but larger pieces can be simmered in water for about ten minutes. You will need ½ cup of water to 1 cup of dried kale.

Celery

Dried celery is not used that often as a vegetable on its own, but the pieces can be used in a number of other recipes to add a little ex-tra flavor. Dry celery piec-es will be hard and crisp when they are done. Pieces should be sliced at least ¼ inch thick.

Dried celery, carrots, and leeks

Dehydrator: Set at 120 F, ten to 16 hours.
Sun drying: Two to three days, in direct sunlight
Oven: Set at 120 F, 18 to 20 hours.
Treatment: No pretreatment is needed for celery.
To rehydrate: Simmer in equal parts water for 25 minutes.

Beets

If you want to preserve the young greens, you can follow the instructions for spinach to dry them. Drying the actual beets is a little more time intensive than the other vegetables. You need to steam or boil the beets for about 20 minutes, then peel off the skin. You can either shred them or dry them in 1/8-inch slices.

Dehydrator: Set at 120 F, eight to ten hours (or four to six for grated beets).
Sun drying: Two to three days for slices, one day for shredded
Oven: Set at 120 F, eight to ten hours (four to six when grated).
Treatment: Just peeling, nothing else is necessary

To rehydrate: Slices can be eaten dry, like a chip, or simmered for just over half an hour. Shredded beets will rehydrate in about 20 minutes the same way.

Leeks

Before you dry leeks, cut away the top and outside leaves, and wash the stalks to get rid of any dirt that was trapped in the tight leaves. Cut into 1/4-inch slices for dehydrating.

Dehydrator: Set to 120 F, 18 to 20 hours.
Sun drying: Three days in full sun
Oven: Set to 120 F, 20 to 28 hours.
Treatment: No need to pretreat leeks
To rehydrate: Simmer in water for about half an hour.

Parsnips

Although they might look a lot like carrots, parsnips certainly taste different, and they dehydrate differently, too. Give them a good scrub, although peeling is not necessary. Slice into 1/8-inch slices, and they will be tough when finished.

Dehydrator: Set at 120 F, eight to 14 hours.

Sun drying: Two to three days in direct sunlight

Oven: Set at 120 F, 12 to 16 hours.

Treatment: Blanch slices in water for about three minutes before drying.

To rehydrate: Simmer 1 cup of parsnip in 2 cups of water for about 40 minutes.

Brussels Sprouts

You only need to cut each one in half before drying, although you can slice thinner if you wish to speed things up. They dry quickly as halves though. Other than blanching, that is all you need to do. If cut into halves, lay them out with the cut sides facing up on your trays. When fully dry, your Brussels sprouts should be brittle to the touch. You might have to cut one open to make sure it is dry right through.

Dehydrator: Set at 120 F, eight to ten hours.

Sun drying: Two to three days in full sun

Oven: Set at 120 F, 16 to 20 hours.

Treatment: Blanch for four or five minutes, and then drain well.

To rehydrate: You need about 1 ½ cups of water for every 1 cup of sprouts. Simmer for 40 minutes.

Artichokes

Remove the tough outside leaves until you are at the tender heart. Slice into ¼-inch pieces. They will need to be blanched first, and when dry, they will be quite brittle. If you do not have fresh artichokes, you can dry canned artichoke hearts. Just add a few more hours to the drying time because there is more moisture in the canned ones.

Dehydrator: Set at 120 F, 14 to 16 hours.

Sun drying: Three days in direct sun

Oven: Set at 120 F, 16 to 18 hours.

Treatment: Steam blanch for six minutes first.

To rehydrate: Simmer for about half an hour, with equal parts artichoke pieces and water.

Seaweed

Although it is not a traditional vegetable, various forms of seaweed are edible, and this is the best place to categorize it. Buying fresh seaweed is not too likely, so this mostly will apply if you live by the coast and are able to harvest your own right from the sea. There are many kinds of edible seaweed, such as kelp, dulse, and nori. You should make sure you can recognize the right varieties before collecting. Rinse it off before bringing your catch home to get rid of any sand, but pat as dry as possible before dehydrating. When dry, most seaweed will be crisp. It can be stored in pieces or ground down for a healthy and nutrient-rich powder.

Dulse seaweed

Dehydrator: Set at 120 F, six to ten hours.

Sun drying: Ten to 14 hours in full sunlight

Oven: Set at 120 F, eight to 12 hours.

Treatment: No treatment required

To rehydrate: Dried seaweed can be crumbled into other dishes or salads; it is not usually rehydrated to eat as a vegetable.

Frozen Mixed Vegetables

If you like to have dried vegetables on hand for cooking or soup mixes but do not really have the time to slice up fresh vegetables, you can save a lot of time by drying frozen. It has been mentioned with corn and peas, though you can use this technique with almost any kind of frozen vegetable. These instructions are for small foods such as corn and anything in small dices. Large pieces also can be dried, although they can take considerably longer. You can just pour your frozen food right on your drying tray without thawing. Remove any large pieces of frost or ice though, as you do not want melted water dripping into the machine.

Dehydrator: Set at 120 F, ten to 14 hours.

Sun drying: Two days

Oven: Set at 120 F, ten to 14 hours.

Treatment: No need to pretreat

To rehydrate: Check the rehydration instructions for the specific type of vegetable. Unless you have some unusual frozen vegetables, just simmer in water until they are soft.

Recipes Using Dried Vegetables

Not too many dried vegetables are eaten while still dry, but rehydrating them to use as a cooked vegetable with meals is a good option. There are countless ways to cook with dried vegetables, sometimes rehydrating first and sometimes just using the dried pieces in the recipe.

Glazed Sweet Potatoes

These sweet potatoes have a thick and zesty sauce to make them a tasty side dish for nearly any meal.

- 3 cups water
- 3 cups sweet potato pieces
- ⅔ cup sugar
- 1 Tbsp. cornstarch
- ½ tsp. orange or lemon zest
- 1 cup orange juice
- 2 Tbsp. butter

Combine the dried sweet potato and water in a saucepan and heat for about 40 minutes at a low simmer. Once done, you can start preheating your oven to 350 F. In a small mixing bowl, stir together the sugar, cornstarch, zest, and juice. Heat this sauce through for several minutes until it is thickened. Stir in butter at this point. In a casserole dish, pour orange sauce over the potatoes, and bake for about 45 minutes. Stir occasionally to make sure all the potato pieces are well covered in sauce. This recipe makes about 4 servings of glazed potatoes.

Vegetable Lasagna

You can make a filling lasagna with several different kinds of dried vegetables for a meal that can feed the whole family. Make sure you get the type of lasagna noodles that can be used dry for this. Because they do not need to be cooked first, they are usually labeled as "no boil" noodles. *Also, mushrooms feature prominently in this recipe; you can find more about drying mushrooms in Chapter 8.*

- 1 cup dried tomato pieces
- 1 cup dried eggplants slices or cubes
- ½ cup dried red sweet pepper slices
- 2 cups boiling water
- 1 cup dried mushrooms
- ½ cup dried onions
- 1 cup boiling water
- 2 eggs
- 1 cup ricotta cheese (or cottage cheese)
- 1 cup dried spinach pieces
- 12 no-boil lasagna noodles
- 5 cups tomato sauce
- 2 cups shredded mozzarella (or a blend of cheeses)

In a large bowl, combine the tomato, eggplant, and pepper pieces in the first measure of hot water. Let it soak for about half an hour. Do the same with the mushrooms and onion in the second measure of water. Drain them both while saving the excess water.

You can start to preheat your oven to 350 F at this point.

Combine the ricotta cheese with eggs and stir until well blended together. Mix in the dried spinach. In another bowl, combine the tomato sauce with 1 cup of the saved water from the vegetables earlier.

In a 13 by 9-inch baking pan, pour about 1 ½ cups of sauce mixture. Add a layer of lasagna noodles (it should take about three of them). Add another 1 ½ cups of sauce, and then a layer of tomatoes, eggplant, and peppers. Add another layer of noodles, then more sauce. Now make a layer with the mushrooms and onions, and then again with more noodles.

Now spread the ricotta cheese mixture, and top with a noodle layer. Cover over with a generous layer of sauce, and top with shredded cheese.

Cover the entire dish with a piece of foil, and bake for 40 minutes. Then take off the foil, and bake for 15 minutes more to brown the cheese. Let it sit for about ten minutes, and then serve.

Creamed Corn Casserole

This recipe makes an excellent side dish to add a little extra flavor to your usual corn kernels.

- 3 cups water
- 1 ½ cups dried corn kernels
- 1 Tbsp. dried sweet pepper
- 2 Tbsp. butter
- 2 Tbsp. flour
- 2 eggs, lightly beaten
- ½ cup bread crumbs

Cook the corn and pepper in water at a simmer for about 50 minutes. Drain, but save the liquid when the corn is soft. If you have less than a cup of liquid, add water to make up a cup's worth and then set aside.

Melt butter in large skillet, and stir in flour once the butter is melted. Slowly pour in the cup of liquid from earlier. Keep the heat at low, and stir constantly. When it starts to thicken, add the eggs, and keep stirring. Finally, mix in the corn and pepper mixture. Once everything is combined, pour out into a casserole dish. Top with bread crumbs, and bake at 350 F for 45 minutes.

Potatoes au Gratin

A classic potato dish can be made quickly even when using dried potatoes.

- 2 cups dried potato slices
- ½ cup dried onion pieces
- 1 ½ Tbsp. vegetable stock powder
- ½ cup bread crumbs
- ¼ cup Parmesan cheese
- 2 cups water

Combine potatoes, onion, and vegetable stock in water and soak at room temperature for half an hour. Then get it simmering over low heat until the potatoes are fully softened. It should only take another 20 minutes. Take the pot from heat, and top with a mixture of bread crumbs and Parmesan. Let it sit for about five minutes, then serve.

Herb and Tomato Sauce

You do not have to use your vegetables only in side dishes and main courses. You can whip up a nice tomato sauce using dried tomatoes. *Drying herbs was covered in Chapter 4 if you plan to use your own for this.*

- 1 tsp. dried garlic (powder or minced pieces)
- 1 cup dried tomatoes
- 2 Tbsp. dried onion
- 1 Tbsp. dried parsley
- 1 tsp. dried basil
- 1 tsp. dried oregano

- ¼ tsp. salt
- ¼ tsp. black pepper
- 4 cups water

Combine everything in a large saucepan, and heat to a boil. Turn down the heat, and let it simmer for about half an hour. Using a blender, purée the whole mixture until it is smooth enough for your liking. If the final sauce is too thin, you can bring it back to a simmer, and let it cook down for another 20 minutes or so until it is thick enough to your taste.

Classic Ratatouille

A mix of vegetables and herbs, this Mediterranean dish makes a hearty casserole that can be used as a main course or side dish.

- ½ cup dried eggplant
- ½ cup dried zucchini
- ¼ cup dried tomatoes, chopped
- 3 Tbsp. dried onion
- 3 Tbsp. dried bell pepper
- ¼ tsp. dried thyme
- 1 tsp. dried basil
- 1 tsp. dried garlic, minced
- Dash of cayenne (if you want the extra heat)
- 2 cups vegetable stock

Combine all ingredients together in a large cooking pot. Heat it until it all begins to boil, and then turn the heat down to a simmer. Stir frequently to keep it from sticking. Simmer for about half an hour or until everything is tender to your liking. Continue cooking if you prefer a thicker consistency to the broth.

Pumpkin Bread

You even can use dried vegetables in many kinds of baked goods, even the sweet ones. This particular recipe will make two loaves of pumpkin bread.

- 1 ½ cups hot water
- 1 ½ cups dried pumpkin pieces
- ⅔ cup shortening
- ⅔ cup sugar
- 4 eggs
- ⅔ cup cold water
- 3 ⅓ cups flour
- 2 tsp. baking soda
- 1 tsp. salt
- ½ tsp. baking powder
- 2 tsp. cinnamon
- 1 tsp. ground cloves
- 1 cup dried apricots, diced (optional)

The dried pumpkin should be in small pieces for this recipe to work the best. Soak pumpkin in hot water for 30 minutes. While that is softening up, you can mix the rest of the batter and preheat the oven to 350 F.

Mix sugar and shortening together in a mixing bowl until smooth and fluffed. Stir in the eggs, softened pumpkin, and the measure of cold water. Beat until well mixed, and then add the flour, baking soda, baking powder, salt, and spices. Mix until everything is combined and moist. Fold in the chopped apricots, and pour batter into two loaf pans.

Bake for about an hour. A toothpick should come out clean when stuck into the center of each loaf.

Cheesy Cauliflower Bake

You can substitute half the cauliflower for dried broccoli (or all of it, for that matter) for a different taste.

- 1 cup dried cauliflower pieces
- 2 Tbsp. dried onion
- 1 cup hot water
- 1 Tbsp. butter
- 2 Tbsp. flour
- 1 ½ cups milk
- 1 cup shredded Cheddar cheese
- 1 tsp. mustard
- 1 cup bread crumbs

Soak cauliflower and onion in hot water for about half an hour. Drain and put the vegetables into a 4-cup baking dish. Once they are softened, you can start preheating your oven to 375 F.

In a small pot, melt butter, and stir in flour to make a smooth paste. Then add milk with a whisk, and keep heating until the mixture starts to bubble. Keep whisking, or it will stick to the bottom of your saucepan. Add ¾ cup of the cheese and the mustard, and whisk until it is all melted and combined. Remove from heat. Pour this sauce over the cauliflower in the baking dish.

Sprinkle the rest of the cheese along with the bread crumbs over top, and bake for 25 minutes until the crust topping has started to brown.

Ham Green Beans

There is not enough ham in this recipe for it to be a main course but just enough to add some rich flavor to your beans. If you do not have ham, you can substitute cooked bacon instead.

- 2 cups dried green beans
- $1/8$ cup dried onion
- $1/8$ cup dried celery
- 3 cups hot water
- $1/2$ cup cooked ham, diced

Let the beans, onion, and celery soak in hot water for about 40 minutes. When that is almost ready, brown the ham in a skillet, and add to the soaked vegetables. You do not need to strain the vegetables for this. Heat the whole thing to a simmer, and let it cook for about half an hour. If it gets too dry, add a little extra water.

Beef and Vegetable Soup

The great thing about this recipe is that you can use any dried vegetables you wish, depending on what you have on hand or just what you prefer in taste. Vegetables such as corn, peas, potatoes, onions, green beans, carrots, celery, zucchini, or turnips all would be suitable in any combination as long as it makes up the total 2 cups.

- 4 beef bouillon cubes
- 2 cups dried vegetables (as listed above)
- $1/4$ cup barley

- ¼ cup dried tomatoes
- 1 bay leaf
- 6 whole peppercorns
- ½ tsp. salt

Combine everything in 2 quarts of water, and simmer in a large stockpot for about an hour until everything has softened up. Remove the bay leaf and peppercorns before serving. You will get about six servings of soup.

Rhubarb and Zucchini Bread

Another great vegetable-based bread that is sweet but with the tart touch of rhubarb as well.

- ¾ cup shredded dried zucchini
- ½ cup dried rhubarb pieces
- 1 ¼ cup water
- 3 eggs
- 1 cup butter
- 2 cups sugar
- 1 tsp. vanilla
- 1 tsp. cinnamon
- ¼ tsp. ground ginger
- ¼ tsp. ground cloves
- 2 ½ cups flour
- 1 tsp. baking powder
- 1 tsp. baking soda
- 1 cup chopped nuts

First, mix the zucchini and rhubarb together with water, and let soak for half an hour. After that, preheat oven to 325 F, and prepare two loaf pans.

Beat eggs with butter, sugar, and vanilla. Mix in the softened zucchini and rhubarb, and then add the spices. In another bowl, mix flour, baking powder, and baking soda together, and pour into the bowl of wet ingredients. Stir until everything is blended, and then fold in the nuts. Pour the batter into your loaf pans, and bake for about an hour. A toothpick should come out clean when it is ready.

Mexican Corn

A little spicy alternative to plain corn kernels as a side dish.

- 2 cups dried corn kernels
- 1 cup dried red or green pepper pieces
- ½ cup dried onion pieces
- 3 ½ cups water
- 1 tsp. cornstarch
- ¼ tsp. salt
- ⅛ tsp. ground black pepper
- A dash of garlic powder

Mix the dried vegetables together with water, and simmer for half an hour or until they are mainly rehydrated. Drain out the excess water, and stir in the cornstarch, salt, pepper, and garlic. Stir through, and put back on the heat for a few minutes until the corn starts to thicken up, and then serve.

Spiced Kale Chips

This recipe is not a way to use dried kale, but rather another way of making dried kale chips (to be eaten dry). Dried kale works well as a chip just naturally as well.

- Fresh kale
- Olive oil
- Spices (paprika, ginger, chili powder, garlic powder)
- Salt

There are no specific measurements for this one, but it is easy enough to estimate on your own. Tear kale into finger-food sized pieces and toss with a little olive oil. Sprinkle your preferred spices until the pieces are well flavored. Then dry the kale pieces as per the instructions earlier in the chapter. You can snack on them just like potato chips.

Okra and Rice

For an okra recipe that is a little easier than making authentic gumbo, try this easy casserole dish of okra and rice.

- 2 ½ cups dried okra
- 2 cups water
- ¾ lb. bacon, cooked and diced
- 1 large onion, chopped
- 1 can chicken broth (15 oz.)
- 1 cup uncooked rice
- 1 ½ cups water

Start by soaking the dried okra in the first measure of water for around half an hour to start them rehydrating. You could cook the bacon at this point.

Strain off the extra water, and set the okra aside. Start to sauté the onion in a large skillet or pan. When it softens, add in bacon, okra, and chicken broth. Cook until the okra is fully rehydrated and soft. Add the additional measure of water with the rice. Simmer for 20 minutes until the rice is fully cooked. Serve while still hot.

Baked Cabbage Casserole

The creamy nature of this dish helps to offset the strong cabbage flavor. It is a great side dish to any meal.

- 6 cups dried cabbage
- 5 cups water
- 1 onion, diced
- 1 ½ cups milk
- 4 eggs, beaten
- 1 cup seasoned bread crumbs
- 1 tsp. salt
- ½ tsp. black pepper

Simmer the cabbage and water until the cabbage is rehydrated. Drain out any extra water, and set aside. Sauté onion in a large saucepan, and when they are soft, add the cabbage. Add the milk, and heat until just boiling. Lower the heat so it is just simmering, and let it cook for about five more minutes.

Stir in the eggs, and then ¾ cup of the bread crumbs and the salt and pepper. Pour everything into a casserole dish, and sprinkle the last ¼ cup of bread crumbs over the top. Bake at 350 F for about half an hour until the top starts to brown.

Carrot Cake

Here is another sweet way to use your dried vegetables — in a classic carrot cake. When making this cake, it is best to use carrots that were dried as  shredded carrots rather than try to grate dried slices of carrots.

- 2 cups grated dried carrots
- 2 cups hot water
- 2 cups white sugar
- ¾ vegetable oil
- 3 eggs
- 1 tsp. vanilla
- ¾ cup milk
- ½ cup shredded coconut
- 1 can crushed pineapple (15 oz.)
- 2 cups flour
- 2 tsp. baking soda
- ½ Tbsp. ground cinnamon
- 1 tsp. salt
- 1 cup chopped pecans

Before you begin, soak the dried carrots in water for about 30 minutes. When they are ready, you can start preheating the oven to 350 F.

In a mixing bowl, combine sugar, oil, eggs, vanilla, and milk. Stir until sugar is dissolved and mixture is smooth. Then add the softened carrots, coconut, and pineapple. Set that aside, and sift together the flour, baking soda, cinnamon, and salt in another bowl. Then add to the wet ingredients mixture. When mixed, fold in the chopped nuts.

Pour batter into a 9 x 13-inch cake pan, and bake for about 50 minutes. A toothpick will come out clean when it is done. Serve warm, or frost with your favorite cream cheese frosting.

Mushrooms and Peas

You do not have to settle for plain peas as a side dish. This simple recipe combines mushrooms, peas, and a little spice.

- 1 cup dried peas
- ½ cup dried mushrooms
- 1 ½ cups water
- 1 small onion, diced
- 2 cloves garlic, minced
- 2 Tbsp. butter
- ½ tsp. salt
- ¼ dried thyme
- Dash of black pepper

Simmer peas, mushrooms, and water together until the vegetables are soft. Drain out the excess water if there is any. In another pan, sauté the onion and garlic with butter. When the onion has started to soften up, add the peas and mushrooms to the pan, and stir through.

Sprinkle the seasonings in, and let cook for a few minutes more. Serve hot. Makes enough for about four servings.

Creamy Broccoli and Potato Soup

There is no actual cream in this soup, but the potatoes thicken it nicely. It is a hearty soup with a lot of flavor.

- 2 cups dried broccoli pieces
- 1 ½ cups dried potato pieces
- 2 cups water
- 1 Tbsp. olive oil
- 1 onion, diced
- 3 cloves garlic, minced
- 4 cups chicken broth
- ¼ tsp. nutmeg

Simmer the broccoli and potato until they begin to soften and the water is absorbed. They will not be fully rehydrated at this point, but that is fine. In another large saucepan, sauté the onion and garlic in oil until the onion is soft. Stir in the broccoli and potatoes and then the chicken broth. Simmer until the broccoli and potatoes are fully soft and cooked.

Use a hand blender to purée the mixture into a smooth soup. Bring it back to a simmer until it is heated through. Serve with a sprinkle of nutmeg. This recipe will make a large batch of soup that will serve six to eight people.

Green Bean Casserole

This is a traditional dish to serve with a holiday meal such as Thanksgiving, and it can be made just as easily with dried beans. It does call for premade stuffing, so you will need that on hand.

- 2 cups dried green beans
- 2 cups water
- 1 cup onion, diced
- 2 Tbsp. butter
- 2 Tbsp. flour
- 1 cup milk
- ¾ shredded Cheddar cheese
- ½ cup sour cream
- ½ tsp. salt
- 2 cups bread stuffing

Let your beans soak in water for about half an hour while they start to soften. When that is done, the oven can be preheated to 350 F, and you can sauté the onions in butter until they are also getting soft. Stir in flour, and then pour in milk while stirring.

Bring the mixture to a boil, and then add cheese, sour cream, and salt. Heat while still stirring until it gets thick.

Drain the green beans and put them into a 9 x 13-inch baking dish. Pour the cheese mixture over the beans, and then add a thick layer of stuffing. Bake for 30 minutes until the top is nicely brown and crisp. This will serve six to eight people.

Cheesy Carrot Casserole

Cheese and carrots is an unusual mix but a good one. You can use either shredded or sliced dry carrots.

- 2 cups dried carrots
- 2 cups water
- 1 Tbsp. butter
- ½ onion, diced
- 1 cup shredded cheese
- ½ green bell pepper, diced
- 2 Tbsp. chopped parsley
- ¼ cup dried bread crumbs

In a cooking pot, simmer water and carrots until thoroughly soft. Start the oven preheating to 350 F, and turn the carrots out into a mixing bowl. Mash them with a fork, and then mix in butter, onion, cheese, pepper, and parsley. Spoon the carrot mixture into a greased baking dish, and then top with bread crumbs.

Bake for 40 minutes until the top starts to brown. This casserole makes about four servings.

Baba Ghanoush

Baba ghanoush is a Middle Eastern dip or spread made with eggplants. It is tasty and easy to make up with dried eggplant, too.

- 1 cup dried eggplant pieces
- ½ cup boiling water
- 3 Tbsp. tahini (sesame paste)
- 1 Tbsp. lemon juice
- 1 Tbsp. olive oil
- 1 tsp. garlic, minced
- ¼ tsp cumin

Soak eggplant in hot water for about 45 minutes until it starts to soften. Drain, and then mix all the ingredients in a blender and process until pureed. Refrigerate to chill before using.

Brussels Sprouts with Bacon

This is a great side dish to make for people who may not like Brussels sprouts all that much. The bacon and nuts complement the flavors nicely.

- 2 cups dried Brussels sprouts
- 3 cups water
- ½ lb. bacon
- ⅔ cup pine nuts (or other nut you prefer)
- 3 green onions, diced
- ½ tsp. seasoned salt

Start simmering your dried Brussels sprouts in water. After about half an hour, cook bacon in a deep pan until it is cooked and crisp. Set the bacon aside, but save the grease in the pan. Over medium heat, cook nuts in bacon grease until they start to brown. Then drain excess water from Brussels sprouts, and add them to the pan. Stir in onion and seasoning. Cook until the sprouts are quite soft, which should be around 15 minutes. Mix in bacon pieces just before you serve.

Asparagus Risotto with White Wine

- 1 cup rice
- ¼ cup dried onion
- 1 tsp. dried garlic, minced
- 4 cups vegetable stock
- ¼ cup white wine
- ½ cup dried asparagus pieces
- 1 tsp. dry lemon zest
- ¼ cup grated Parmesan cheese

In a large skillet or saucepan, combine everything except the Parmesan. Bring to a boil; then reduce the heat down to a simmer. Let it cook for about 20 minutes to half an hour, stirring often. You may need to add extra water if it goes dry before the rice is thoroughly cooked. Let sit for about five minutes off heat to thicken up, and then stir in Parmesan cheese right before serving.

Indian Spiced Parsnips

You can make this with just parsnips or make the same recipe with a mixture of parsnips and carrots to change the flavor.

- 1 ½ cups dried parsnip pieces
- 3 cups water
- 1 tsp. olive oil
- 1 garlic clove, minced
- 1 Tbsp. red wine vinegar
- ½ tsp. paprika
- ¼ tsp. cumin
- Salt and pepper to taste

Simmer parsnip in water for about 35 minutes. Then drain, and set aside. In a skillet, heat oil and sauté garlic for about two minutes. Then stir in the remaining ingredients, and continue to cook for another two to three minutes. Add parsnips, and stir to get the pieces well covered in the sauce. Continue cooking at medium heat until the parsnips are hot through.

Hoppin' John

This is a traditional beans and rice dish popular in the southern U.S. It uses dry black-eyed peas. It is good luck if you serve this on New Year's Day. You can omit the red pepper flakes if you do not want the extra heat.

- 1 ½ cups dry black-eyed peas
- 1 lb. ham hocks (or bacon)
- 1 onion, diced
- ½ tsp. red pepper flakes
- 4 cups water
- 1 ½ cups long-grain rice
- 1 cup sharp Cheddar cheese, grated

In a large pot, pour water over peas, ham hock, onion, and pepper flakes. Bring it all to a boil, and then turn it down to simmer. Cook for an hour and a half. Cut the meat from the hocks, and mix back in. Add the rice, and continue to cook until the rice is ready. It should take another half hour at this point. Serve topped with a generous sprinkling of cheese.

BBQ Lima Beans

These types of recipes are usually made with brown beans or kidney beans, but using lima beans adds a new flavor. This recipe does take a few hours to make, so plan ahead.

- ½ lb. dry lima beans
- 3 cups water
- 1 cup onion, diced
- ½ tsp. salt
- ½ cup ketchup
- ¼ cup brown sugar
- 2 Tbsp. maple syrup
- 3 strips of bacon, cooked and crumbled

In a large pot, cover lima beans with water (about 2 inches over), and bring it to a boil. Note: this is not the 3 cups of water listed in the ingredients. Let the beans boil for about three or four minutes, and then take the pot off the heat. Cover, and let sit for an hour to soak.

Drain the beans, and give them a good rinse. Put them back in the pot with the measured 3 cups of water. Add onions and salt. Bring it back to a boil, and then down to a simmer. Cook for another hour or more until the beans are soft. Drain the beans, and then add the remaining ingredients. Spoon everything to a 2-quart baking dish, and bake at 350 F for half an hour covered. Remove the lid, and then bake for another 30 minutes.

Curry and Cauliflower Soup

This chunky and spicy soup has an unusual mix of flavors. It is also a good way to use several different types of dried vegetables at once.

- 1 Tbsp. curry paste
- 2 cups dried cauliflower pieces
- ½ cup dried celery slices
- ½ cup dried onion pieces
- ½ cup garbanzo beans, canned or soaked

- 8 cups vegetable stock
- ½ cup apple juice
- Salt and pepper to taste

In a large skillet or stockpot, sauté the curry paste until it starts to melt and gets aromatic. Then add in the remaining ingredients. Bring everything to a boil, and then reduce heat to a simmer. Let cook for half an hour until everything is tender; then it is ready to serve.

Sweet and Sour Beets

Beets make a bright and colorful side to any meal, and this recipe is a nice combination of sweet and sour flavors.

- 1 cup dried beet slices
- 1 cup vegetable broth
- 1 Tbsp. olive oil
- ½ cup diced onion
- 1 clove garlic, minced
- 1 Tbsp. flour
- 1 cup vegetable broth
- 2 Tbsp. brown sugar
- ⅓ cup cider vinegar

Simmer beets in first measure of broth for about half an hour. When they are getting soft, sauté onion and garlic in oil for a minute or two. Sprinkle the flour over, and stir until blended with the liquid butter. Add the second measure of broth along with the beets, sugar, and vinegar. Heat until it starts to boil, then turn the heat down to keep it simmering. Keep cooking for an additional ten minutes.

Acorn Squash Soup

You can adjust this recipe to use any other types of winter squash or even pumpkin. It is a pureed soup, so it is thick and perfect for a fall meal.

- 2 cups dried squash pieces
- 2 cups water
- 1 small onion, diced
- ¼ cup celery, diced
- 2 Tbsp. butter
- 2 Tbsp. flour
- 1 cube of chicken bouillon
- ½ tsp. dried dill
- ¼ tsp. curry powder
- 2 cups chicken broth
- 1 can evaporated milk (12 oz.)

Start by simmering the squash and water until your squash is just starting to get soft. In a large stockpot, sauté onion and celery in butter until the onion gets tender. Mix in flour, bouillon powder, dill, and curry until blended together. Slowly pour in the chicken broth and milk. Stir through, and bring the heat up to a boil for a few minutes before adding the squash.

Continue heating at a simmer or more until the squash finishes rehydrating and is getting soft. Now you can either use an immersion blender to puree the soup right in the pot, or pour it (in stages) to a blender to do the same. Either way, the soup should be back in the pot after blending so it can reheat before serving.

Bean and Beef Chili

With so many recipes call-
ing for canned beans, it can
be hard to find good ideas
for using your dried beans
instead. This recipe needs a
slow cooker, which is a great
way of cooking any type of
dried bean.

- 1 lb. ground beef
- 10 cups beef broth
- ¼ tsp. black pepper
- 2 carrots, sliced
- 1 stalk celery, sliced
- 4 oz. dried pinto beans
- 4 oz. dried navy beans
- 4 oz. dried kidney beans
- 6 dried tomatoes, chopped
- Grated Parmesan cheese

Cook beef in a skillet until it is cooked and browned. Skim off as
much fat as you can. Then combine meat, broth, pepper, carrots,
celery, and beans in a slow cooker (at least 5 quarts in size). Cook
on low for seven to eight hours or on high for four to five. At
that point, add the tomatoes, and keep cooking for about another
hour. When the beans are soft, it is ready to serve. Top each bowl
with a handful of grated cheese. *If you are looking for more recipes that include dry beans, try Chapter 12, which has several dry soup
mixes that have dry beans in them.*

Growing Your Own Vegetables

More people are familiar with growing vegetables than fruit, so this is likely not as unusual, even to a novice gardener or people who have never grown their own food.

Nearly all vegetables (except asparagus and rhubarb) are annuals, so you will have to plant new seeds every spring. Because you do not have to overwinter your plants as you do with fruit, your growing region is less important. Each type of vegetable will need a certain amount of growing season, so how long you have consistent warm weather is more important than how cold it gets in the winter.

In areas with a short summer, you can extend your growing season by either starting your plants indoors or by buying seedlings instead of planting seeds. You just have to make sure your plants are not planted outdoors until you have no more chance of frost.

Vegetables are prone to insect damage, so you will want to have a good supply of insecticidal sprays around that are natural and safe to use on food plants. Any sprays with pyrethrum will be effective without adding any toxins to your food.

Many vegetables will produce better if kept upright with supports. Vining plants like cucumber or zucchini can grow on trellis, and shorter plants such as tomatoes can be kept up in a tomato cage or tied to a stake.

Cucumbers, green beans, tomatoes, carrots, and peas are easy vegetables to start with. Peas grow quickly and would give the earliest harvest, but the others will take a few months before you can start picking. When growing vegetables for dehydrating, try to plan your drying time as soon as possible after you have picked them. If you have to save up several days' worth in order to fill your dehydrator, store the extra in the fridge until you are ready to use them.

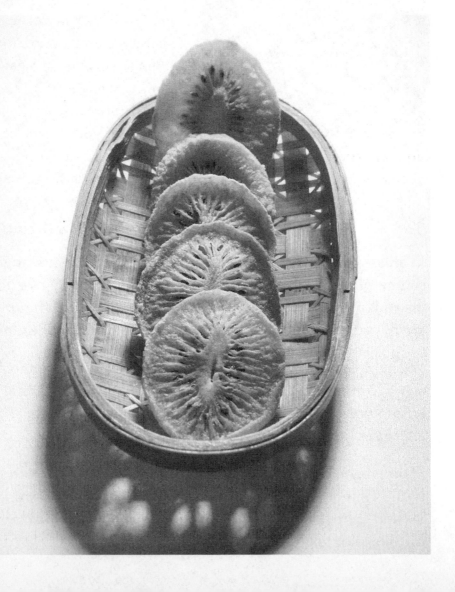

Chapter 7

LEATHERS
AND ROLLS

U p until now, the instructions have only been for drying whole pieces of each fruit, vegetable, and herb. But there are other ways of dehydrating to produce other types of results.

What are Leathers?

Before you learn more on how to make them, it would be helpful to have a better understanding of what fruit or vegetable leather is.

Leathers are made by dehydrating a layer of fruit or vegetable purée until it is pliable, just like a piece of leather. Fruit is the most common type of leather, although you certainly can experiment and make some interesting ones out of vegetables as well. They usually are eaten as is, a handy snack, although you can use your leathers as a way to preserve food for other uses as well.

Fruit leather can be purchased as a children's treat or snack, usually called a "fruit roll-up" or something similar. These are made with fruit but also contain a great deal of sugar. You can make your own with pure fruit that taste just as good if not better. When wrapped in wax paper, they are just as portable as any store-bought versions.

Photo courtesy of Douglas and Sherri Brown

Making Leather

There is more processing involved in making leather than just washing and chopping your fruits and vegetables for the dehydrator.

Preparing fruits and vegetables for leathers

One of the great things about making leather is that you can make use of any produce that is too ripe for conventional dehydrating. Once they have gotten too soft, most fruits will not dry well as slices, but they can be turned into wonderful leather instead.

Your fruit is going to be puréed; so, you do not need to worry about accurate slicing or chopping. Just remove any bruises, brown spots, and stems before you begin. Most fruits and vegetables are peeled if they have a tough peel, but softer foods will not need that step.

Some fruits can be puréed raw, and some may be cooked. Both will dry well into leather, but the taste will be different. *The specific details will be covered in the next section.*

Leather-making methods

Once your produce is cleaned up, you will need to make a purée. Cooked foods will purée more easily, but just about any fruit or vegetable will purée in a blender, even when raw. Harder vegetables, such as carrots, will be smoother if you cook them first.

Photo courtesy of Douglas and Sherri Brown

Your purée needs to be thin enough to be pourable; so, add extra water or fruit juice to thin it out if necessary. There is no precise way to measure the right consistency. It may take a few trial runs to see how well it dries. You will need roughly 2 cups to fill an average dehydrator, but you can always adjust this to suit how much room you have to dry with.

Specific recipes will come later in this chapter, but be aware that you can mix any fruits and vegetables together when making your purées. There is no need to keep everything separate. Unlike dehydrating other types of fruit and vegetables, there is no difference in drying times once puréed. So, any kind of leather will take the same time to dry regardless of what kind of food you have used as the ingredients.

Spread your purée on a sheet of wax paper cut to fit the trays in your dehydrator. It should be no thicker than ⅛ inch, although it can be tough to measure a puddle of purée accurately. Thinner layers will dry faster, but you can end

Photo courtesy of Douglas and Sherri Brown

up with it stuck to the wax paper if it is not thick enough to hold together when you go to peel it back. It will take about 12 hours to dry your leather at a temperature of 120 F. You should dry your leather pieces for about six hours. Then peel from the paper, flip over each piece, and continue to dry until neither side is sticky.

You also can use the sun to make leather, but the sticky nature of the purée does make it hard to keep your trays clean. Insects and debris will be a constant problem. Set your trays up some place in full sun where they will not be disturbed, and cover them with cheesecloth. Line with wax paper again, and dry the same way as in a dehydrator, except flip over the pieces after one day of drying. Continue for another full day after that.

Last, you also can use your oven to dry leathers. Use a paper-lined baking sheet, and set your oven to 120 F. As with the other methods, you will have to peel your leather from the paper half-way through so it dries properly. In the oven, it will be about eight hours before you flip it and another eight hours after.

You cannot safely make fruit or vegetable leather with simple air drying. The liquid state of the purée will mold too quickly for this to work.

The biggest challenge with making leather is having it stick to your trays or sheets of paper. A light brushing of oil on your wax paper can help. Also, you will have a better time of removing the paper if you flip it over so the drying leather is on the bottom, and then peel the paper back. It works better than trying to peel the leather off directly.

Storing leathers

As long as your pieces of leather are no longer sticky, they will last many months. The easiest way to store them is to keep them on their wax paper backing and roll them up. You can use scissors to cut both the leather and the paper to make the tubes the right size for a container.

Properly dried fruit or vegetable leather can be stored at room temperature, although you also can store it in the fridge if you prefer the cool taste when eating it as a snack.

Recipes for Making Leathers

Because the actual technique is going to be primarily the same no matter what kind of leather you are making, these recipes are more about options for mixing various fruit and vegetable combinations together to create new flavors.

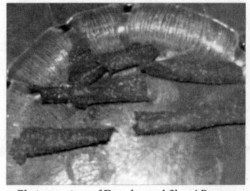

Photo courtesy of Douglas and Sherri Brown

On the other hand, there are also a few examples of leathers you can make for rehydrating later. In those cases, further instructions are included.

You also can use yogurt to make a creamier type of leather. *Look to Chapter 11 on dairy for instructions on yogurt leathers.*

Spiced Apple Leather

You can make plain apple leather with just fruit and juice, but the addition of a few spices can really improve the flavor.

- 4 apples
- ½ cup water or apple juice
- ¼ tsp. cinnamon
- ⅛ tsp. cloves

Chop and cook the apples until soft; then combine everything in a blender or food processor to purée. Dry by your preferred method. You can substitute store-bought applesauce for this recipe as long as you have about 2 cups worth. You will not need any extra water or juice in that case.

Banana and Chocolate Leather

Maybe not quite as healthy as the all-fruit mixtures, but a little chocolate goes well with the mellow flavor of banana.

- 4 bananas (very ripe is best)
- 2 Tbsp. cocoa powder
- 1 Tbsp. white sugar

Mash or purée bananas, and mix in cocoa and sugar until it is all combined and smooth. Dry until no longer tacky or sticky.

Mango Strawberry Leather

A vibrant mix of tart fruits will make a tasty snack leather.

- 1 cup chopped mango
- 1 cup strawberries

You also can adjust the ratio if you prefer one flavor to the other. Purée until smooth and dry.

Bumble Berry Leather

A little bit of everything for a summer-fresh mix of fruit.

- ¼ cup strawberries
- ¼ cup blackberries
- ¼ cup blueberries
- ¼ cup raspberries

Purée everything, and dry as per the standard instructions. You might want to put the mixture through a food mill or fine strainer to remove extra seeds.

Tropical Fruit Leather

- 1 cup papaya chunks
- 1 cup pineapple chunks
- 1 large banana

Pineapple can be a little fibrous for this; so, make sure you run it through the blender enough to really have a smooth purée.

Sweet Apple Berry Leather

Fruit on its own is usually quite sweet, but this leather adds a little honey to make an even sweeter treat. There is a nice blend of different fruits and some spice.

- 3 cups chopped raw apples
- 1 cup raspberries
- 3 Tbsp. orange juice
- 2 Tbsp. honey
- 1 tsp. cinnamon
- ½ tsp. lemon juice

Combine the berries and apples, and then blend until smooth. Stir in the remaining ingredients, and dehydrate into leather. This makes a larger batch than the other recipes, so you may have to load up your dehydrator twice.

Peach and Pear Leather

- 1 cup chopped peaches
- 1 cup chopped pears
- ½ tsp. cinnamon or allspice

Use a blender to puree this until smooth, and then dehydrate like the others.

Tomato Sauce Leather

Here is a good example of non-fruit leather that is not supposed to be eaten as a snack in its dry form. This recipe is a dried tomato sauce that can be remade into sauce by heating again in water.

- 2 cups of your favorite tomato or spaghetti sauce

No other ingredients are required, and you can use either store-bought or homemade sauces for this. If you are using a chunky sauce, run it through the blender before drying to make sure you have an even consistency. Then just dry as you would any fruit leathers. Store it the same way as well.

When you want to make tomato sauce with your leather, just combine equal parts water and pieces of leather and simmer until it has all dissolved.

Sweet Potato Leather

The natural sweetness of sweet potatoes makes them a unique vegetable, and when made into leather, it can be eaten as a healthy

snack. You also can stir pieces of sweet potato leather into soups or casseroles to add a little bit of extra nutrients without having to cook more sweet potatoes.

- 2 cups cooked sweet potatoes

Purée until smooth and dry. Because it is starchier than fruit and most other vegetables, it might take longer to dry than usual. A better timing would be eight hours, flip over, and then dry for another eight hours.

Pumpkin Pie Leather

Here is a tasty one for the fall that uses vegetables but is still as sweet as fruit leather.

- ½ cup applesauce
- 2 cups pumpkin purée
- 1 tsp. cinnamon
- ½ tsp. ginger
- ¼ tsp. nutmeg
- ¼ tsp. cloves
- 1 Tbsp. molasses
- 2 Tbsp. brown sugar

Mix ingredients, and dry as per the fruit leather instructions. If you are using chunky applesauce, you might want to run it through the blender so you have a smoother mixture. You can eat this leather dry as a snack.

Chapter 8

DRYING MUSHROOMS

Because mushrooms are neither a fruit nor a vegetable, and because they are ingredients in so many delicious recipes, they really deserve their own section. They dry well and can be part of your overall dehydration plan.

Gathering Wild Mushrooms

Before this chapter can begin, it is only safe to present a clear warning when it comes to harvesting any wild mushrooms. Although it may be tempting to gather "free" food in the wild, you are taking a sizable risk unless you are already extremely familiar with wild mushrooms. The differences between many deadly varieties and those that are edible are minor, and it is easy to confuse them. And making a mistake can be lethal. Never assume you are risking only a stomachache with wild mushrooms.

The toxins present in some species of mushrooms will remain even after they have been thoroughly dehydrated. Having them dried will not make them any safer to eat.

A good field guide can be helpful, especially one designed to illustrate the differences between edible and dangerous species of mushrooms. But even the best field guide can be flawed; photos may not be enough to make the differences clear to you. If you intend to harvest wild mushrooms, it is a good idea to get some personal training from an expert.

Preparing Mushrooms to Be Dried

Mushrooms are not like your typical vegetables, so you will want to know more about them so they can be prepared properly before you begin dehydrating.

Harvesting or buying mushrooms to be dried

The majority of people who dry mushrooms do so with store-bought produce because of the difficulty in growing mushrooms. It is possible, and that will be covered briefly at the end of this chapter in case you do decide to grow your own.

When at the store, look for mushrooms that are firm and plump. If the area where the cap and stalk meet (called the veil) has opened up, it means the mushroom is old and should not be bought.

Unlike most other fruits and vegetables, you only will have success with dehydrating fresh mushrooms. Canned mushrooms should not be used for drying. If you buy them sliced and packaged, you can bypass one step.

Mushrooms will go bad quickly, so when you plan to do some dehydrating, buy your mushrooms only a couple of days beforehand, if not the day of.

Cleaning and preparing mushrooms

You usually can dry an entire mushroom, but some larger ones can have woody stalks you can cut away if you wish. Otherwise,

just remove any browned spots with a knife.

Unless they are dirty, do not wash your mushrooms. Their spongy nature means they will absorb water easily, and that is not what you want when preparing to dehydrate them. Give them a good rubdown or a dry scrub with a vegetable brush. When you are waiting for your dehydrating session, store your mushrooms in a brown paper bag in the refrigerator. This will help release any additional moisture and help your dehydrating when you do get the mushrooms out for drying.

Mushrooms will give up their moisture easily, so you do not have to cut your pieces too thinly. Small mushrooms can be dried whole, otherwise slice into ½-inch pieces. When they dry, they will shrink by a factor of eight to ten (become up to ten times smaller) so do not cut your pieces too small. You will end up with a tray of slivers that are difficult to use.

Additional preparations

There really are not any other steps you need to take when drying mushrooms. They do not need any pretreatment or blanching like fruits or vegetables do. Mushrooms will darken slightly as they dry, but there is nothing you can do to prevent that.

If you are going to dry small pieces, you might want to line your dehydrator trays with cheesecloth to prevent the bits from falling through as they shrink.

Methods for Drying Mushrooms

Mushrooms will dehydrate well overall, and you can choose any method for drying them that suits you the best.

Sun drying mushrooms

Because they are not as sweet or juicy as so many fruits and vegetables, mushrooms dry better outdoors because they will not at-

tract the attention of insects and pests. Lay them out on trays and either leave them exposed or cover with a light layer of cheesecloth. Because they are not sticky, debris is less of a problem.

Mushrooms will have a strong smell when they are dehydrating, so many people prefer outdoor sun drying just to keep the smell out of the house. This is just a matter of personal preference. Because you will want to change the temperature during drying, using the sun can be a little more difficult, although leaving your mushrooms to dry at one temperature is also fine. *There will be more on the specific times and temperatures later in the chapter.*

Air drying mushrooms

Though they do dry well, mushrooms will start to mold quickly, and regular air drying without heat will not dry them quickly enough to avoid mold or mildew contamination. This really is not a method you should choose for working with mushrooms. Stick to the other methods if you can.

Dehydrating mushrooms

Using a commercial dehydrator works well with mushrooms, except for the aroma problem that was mentioned in the section on sun drying.

To best dry mushrooms, you will need to turn up the heat after they have started drying, which makes a dehydrator that comes with temperature controls useful. If your machine does not allow for these types of control measures, you have to adjust the timing. *Check the section below on specific drying instructions for more details.*

Oven drying mushrooms

The oven works quite well for drying mushrooms, as long as you can lower the temperature enough. Best results require that you start drying at lower than 100 F, which most ovens cannot do. But just like with sun drying, you can probably make do if you adjust the times to suit your equipment. A little experimentation can help.

Mushrooms are 90 percent water, so yours will give off a lot of moisture during drying. Leave the oven door open, or it will get so humid inside that they will not finish drying regardless of the temperature.

Storing Dry Mushrooms

Dried mushrooms will not need any unique or special storage. Any container with a tight lid will work, and they should be stored out of direct sunlight. A cupboard or cabinet is better than being displayed on an open kitchen shelf, for example.

As long as they have been dried sufficiently, your mushrooms will last for many months if not years.

Specific Drying Instructions for Mushrooms

Unlike the other sections, there are not going to be specific times and temperatures set out for each type of mushroom. The differences from one type to another are so minor (from a dehydrating perspective) that it makes it unnecessary. You can take these instructions and apply them to Shiitake mushrooms, morels, chanterelles, Porcini mushrooms, or the common white mushrooms. They all will dry the same.

Dried shitake mushrooms

Dehydrator: First dry at 90 F for about three hours, then turn
up the heat to 120 F for another eight to ten hours.
If you cannot adjust the temperature, it will take
about ten to 12 hours without making any adjust-
ments.

Sun drying: One to two days in the full sun

Oven: Same as for the standard dehydrator, though few ovens
will operate as low as 90 F.

Treatment: None needed for mushrooms

To rehydrate: They will soften up quickly and just need to soak
in water (no simmering necessary) for about 30
to 40 minutes. Use a lot of water (at least three
times the amount of mushrooms). If they absorb
it all before they are soft, add more. Because they
shrink so much when drying, they will grow just
as much when the water is added back. So use a
large enough bowl or pot to hold a volume about
ten times what you start with.

Recipes for Dried Mushrooms

Mushrooms will regain their meaty texture when rehydrated, so
they work well in a number of dishes. Because they rehydrate so
quickly, you often just can add them to a pot of soup or a casserole, and they will soften up without any special treatment as the
rest of the pot cooks.

These recipes are for mushrooms in general, and you can use
whatever variety you prefer unless the recipe specifically states
that a certain type of mushroom should be used.

Basic Mushroom Cream Sauce

An easy place to start is a classic mushroom and cream sauce.

- 1 cup dried mush-room pieces
- 3 Tbsp. butter
- 2 Tbsp. water
- 1 cup half and half cream
- 3 Tbsp. water
- 1 Tbsp. flour
- Salt and pepper to taste

In a cook pot, melt the butter along with the water until liquid, and stir in the mushrooms. Continue to heat until they start to soften up. Be prepared to add a little water if the bottom starts to go dry. Stir in the cream, and simmer for about five minutes. In another bowl, blend the second measure of water with flour until it is smooth, then slowly add the mixture to the sauce while stirring. Heat through for another five minutes at a low simmer until the mushrooms are fully rehydrated, and the sauce has thickened up.

Mushroom Risotto

This was initially a camping recipe; so, all the ingredients are dried and convenient to have on hand. You will get enough for two to four people.

- 1 cup dried mushrooms
- 2 cups long-grain rice
- 3 cups of water
- ¼ cup instant vegetable stock powder
- 1 Tbsp. dried parsley

- 2 tsp. dried thyme
- ½ tsp. black pepper
- ½ tsp. garlic powder

Combine all ingredients together in a saucepan and bring to a boil. Once boiling, reduce the heat down to a simmer, and let it cook for about half an hour or until the rice is cooked and the mushrooms are soft. If it begins to get dry in the pot, add additional water.

Mushroom Soup

This makes a creamy soup that would go well with some bread on a winter's day. You will get about four bowls of soup with this recipe.

- 1 cup dried mushroom pieces
- 1 cup boiling water
- 1 beef bouillon cube
- 2 Tbsp. dried onion pieces
- 2 cups water
- 2 Tbsp. cornstarch
- ⅛ tsp. black pepper
- ½ tsp. dried thyme
- 1 can evaporated milk
- ½ cup grated cheese

First, you need to start your mushrooms softening by letting them soak in the first measure of water for about 15 minutes. Do not drain them, but put the mushrooms and remaining water in a saucepan over medium heat. Add the bouillon and onion, and then stir in the second measure of water. Keep heating until it reaches a boil, and then bring back down to a simmer. Cook while stirring often for about five more minutes.

Then add the cornstarch, pepper, and thyme while you continue to heat the soup. When it starts to thicken, pour in the evaporated milk. When you are ready to serve, top each bowl with a generous sprinkle of grated cheese.

Sautéed Mushrooms with Herbs

Not all mushroom recipes have to be creamy. This is a savorier mix of herbs for your dried mushrooms.

- 2 ½ cups dried mushrooms
- 2 cups water
- 2 Tbsp. butter
- 2 Tbsp. onion, diced
- 2 tsp. dried tarragon
- ½ tsp. nutmeg
- ¼ tsp. salt
- ⅛ tsp. black better

Simmer mushrooms in water for about 20 minutes or until they are mostly rehydrated. Drain off any excess water, and transfer mushrooms to a skillet. Add butter, and heat until the butter is melted and starting to sizzle a little. Stir in the rest of the ingredients, and cook mushrooms until they are fully soft and cooked. Makes side dish servings for about four.

Marinated Mushrooms

This appetizer will work best if you have larger pieces of dried mushrooms to work with, but anything can work. Serve before a meal or as an elegant side dish.

- 1 cup dried mushrooms
- 1 cup water
- 1 onion, diced
- ¾ cup olive oil
- ¼ cup vinegar
- 2 cloves minced garlic
- ½ tsp. salt
- ¼ tsp. dry mustard
- ⅛ tsp. black pepper

Combine water and mushrooms in a small saucepan, and simmer until the mushrooms have rehydrated. Drain them, and let them cool.

Toss the mushrooms with the rest of the ingredients, and let it all steep in the refrigerator overnight before serving cold the next day.

Penne Pasta and Mushrooms

The meaty texture of mushrooms is a great addition to a simple pasta dish.

- ½ cup dried mushrooms
- ½ cup water
- 1 cup penne pasta
- ¼ cup olive oil
- 1 clove minced garlic
- 1 Tbsp. butter

- 2 tsp. fresh parsley
- ¼ grated Parmesan cheese

Simmer mushrooms in water for about 15 to 20 minutes, and then drain and set aside. While that is cooking, you also can cook the pasta in another pot of water. Sauté the garlic in olive oil, then add the mushrooms, and cook for several more minutes until they are fully cooked. Add butter, and stir in until melted. Pour the mushroom mixture over the pasta, and top with parsley and cheese before serving.

Growing Your Own Mushrooms

Growing mushrooms is not a common pursuit, and you might be surprised to hear that it is something you can do at home. Although it would be a good idea to be somewhat familiar with gardening if you are going to try this, it is not necessary because conventional gardening knowledge is not going to help. Growing your own mushrooms is a whole other ball game.

If this is something you want to try, you can purchase kits from gourmet food shops or specialty gardening stores that will provide you with all the materials and instructions you need. Once you get the hang of it, you can buy your supplies without the added expense of the kit.

Mushrooms do not have seeds but rather grow from tiny spores. When buying material to start your own mushrooms, you can either use these or preprocessed little plugs that are made of spores and pressed sawdust. They are called "spawn" and are much easier to handle than the loose powdery spores.

The specific details on how to raise mushrooms is too detailed to explain completely here, but the general idea is that the spawn are inserted into a proper growing medium (such as a wooden log, or packed straw and sawdust). Once the log or other material is "inoculated," you need to protect it and keep it in a dark location where you can turn up the temperature. Most mushrooms will start to form after about a month.

Your biggest risk with growing your own mushrooms is that your growing medium ends up catching natural wild mushroom spores in the area. These can grow into deadly mushrooms, so you need to have your growing area indoors where you can limit the exposure to outside air.

CASE STUDY:
HOMEGROWN AND
WILD-HARVESTED

Naomi Lever
Little Carlton,
Louth Lincolnshire LN11 8HP
www.facebook.com/groups/
Backyardfarming

Not only does Naomi use her old seven-tray stackable dehydrating unit to dry fruits and herbs, she also takes advantage of the warm dry air around her wood stove to do even more dehydrating.

In the dehydrator, she dries all kinds of fruit including some that she harvests wild from around her home. Dried elderberries are an important ingredient for her wine making, for example. With the stove, she strings up apple rings and chili peppers. Overall, her favorite foods to dry are mushrooms, apples, pears, plums, and all the herbs. She finds the dried fruit to be a wonderful healthy snack for her children.

She has been doing dehydrating at home for nearly ten years (on and off), and she has gained a lot of valuable experience along the way. The only thing she has never tried to dehydrate is wild mushrooms mainly because she is not confident about harvesting only the safe varieties.

She also does not dry meat because she seldom eats meat in the first place.

When doing fruits, she reminds people to slice everything as evenly as possible so the slices will dry consistently. Before drying, Naomi also dips much of her fruit in lemon juice to keep it from going brown. Potatoes also get a dipping before she dries. Naomi's dried produce is kept in tightly sealed glass jars.

Chapter 9

GRAINS, NUTS, AND BREAD

You are now fully versed in drying fruits, vegetables, herbs, and mushrooms. But you still are going to be able to use a number of other foods in your dehydrator. These have been grouped together here even though they represent a number of different types of food.

Dehydrating Grains

Grains are not something the average person would grow at home, and when buying grains in the store, they are already dried. But knowing how to handle these types of foods can still be important if you want to have a well-rounded knowledge of food dehydration.

This section does not include any recipes because regular store-bought grains are already dried, so there is no need to learn any new cooking techniques to use your home-dried grains.

Harvesting and preparing grains

Buying undried grains is mostly unheard of, so the only way you will have grains around to dry is if you have grown them your-

self. Just because it is not common certainly does not mean it is difficult. *There is more information at the end of this section on how to grow your own grains if you want to try it.*

Barley

When planning to harvest your own grains, it is typi-cal to let the seeds dry right on the stalks before you harvest, so the dehydrating requirements are minimal. When the stalks are dry with the seeds coming loose, you can slice off the seed heads and collect them carefully so as not to spill any seeds. Wheat, oats, barley, rye, and many others are collected this way.

Once they are gathered, you have to beat them enough to get the seeds loose from the stalks. It is called threshing. A good way to do it on a small scale is to bundle your grains up in a pillowcase and beat with a broom handle. Once you have it all threshed, then you separate the seeds from the leftover stalk pieces.

Again, that can be an easy process. Just slowly pour the material from a few feet in the air in front of a fan. The breeze will blow the bits of stalk, and the grains themselves will drop down to be collected. This step is called winnowing. It might seem complicated, but both steps are actually simple and can be done with a minimum of equipment.

Also, although many people consider corn to be part of the grains family, it has been considered a vegetable for the purpose of this book and can be found in that chapter.

Methods for drying grains

Because you left the grain to dry on the stalk for the most part, you are already starting with dry material. Even so, the tough nature of a grain seed makes air drying impractical. Sun, oven, or dehydrator will all work just fine.

The small size of most grains can pose a problem if you are using either a sun drying or a proper dehydrator. You must cover trays that are left outside, or you can lose your grains to the wind or to hungry birds. With dehydrators, the problem can come from your slotted or mesh trays. Something as small as a rye seed might fall through. A layer or two of cheesecloth under your grains is usually fine. If you intend to do a lot of grain drying, you might want to take some time to cut stainless steel window screening to fit in your dehydrator trays (just do not use anything galvanized because it will leach toxic materials to your food).

There really are no special considerations for doing oven drying, but it is another option.

Storing dried grains

Storing home-dried grains is no different than storing any grains you have purchased from the store in the past. Any container with a tight-fitting lid will suffice as long as it does not let any light in. Otherwise, you have to make sure you store your dried grains in a dark place.

If you are doing your own grain harvesting, there is always a slight risk of tiny insect eggs getting into your grains while you are doing your threshing and winnowing. Even the heat of the drying process will not kill *all* these eggs, and they can hatch once in storage. One or two insects in a container of grain can ruin the entire batch. To help prevent this, put your dried grain in the freezer for at least 24 hours (48 would be better) before you put the container away in the cupboard. This should help kill any remaining pest eggs in your grains. When using the sun for drying, this is a more important step because the grains are not heated as much during the dehydration process.

Dry wheat grains

Instructions for drying grains

Details such as time and temperature are going to be the same no matter what kind of small grain you are drying, so there is no need to expand out the instructions for every type of grain or seed. This will work just fine for wheat, rye, barley, oats, or whatever you are growing.

> *Dehydrator:* Set at 115 F, 12 to 16 hours.
> *Sun drying:* Dry grains in the sun for one to two days, left in full sunlight
> *Oven:* Set at 115 F, 18 to 20 hours
> *Treatment:* Nothing is necessary once the grains are threshed and winnowed
> *To rehydrate:* Grains are seldom rehydrated for use, and any recipes that call for these types of grains already assumes they will be dried.

These drying times are estimates because it will highly depend on how dry your grains are when you harvest them from the plants.

Growing your own grains

Growing any of the small grains listed in the above sections is actually quite easy to do yourself. Each specific type of grain will have its own growing requirements, but a few things are common to growing any of them.

Grains typically are grown in large quantities, but you do not have to have acres of fields in order to grow a little on your own. You can get five to ten bushels of grains from just a quarter of an acre. For one family to dry, that is a lot of grain. The exact yield will depend on what you are growing and what your local growing conditions are.

These plants all grow similarly to tall grasses and will have a seed head of some sort at the top of the stalk. You usually do not grow grains in ordered rows because the plants are so thin. Instead, spread the seed out over the soil, and let it all grow. Once the plants begin to come, you will not have to do much weeding because they will be tall and you will not have space between plants for you to do so anyway.

You just sow the seed and make sure it is watered through the season. They are self-sufficient plants that do not require a lot of direct care on your part.

At harvest time, you need to watch for the seeds to develop and start to dry on the plant. Once you cut the seeds off each grain stalk, you will have to process them as described in the "Harvesting and Preparing" section above.

These plants are annuals and need to be reseeded each year, although some seeds will drop from your stalks during harvest. You may find that your patch of grains will naturally reseed itself.

Dehydrating Nuts and Seeds

Just like with grains, the nuts you purchase usually are going to be either dried or roasted already. This means that if you want

to do any dehydrating, it will most likely be with raw nuts you have grown yourself.

Sunflower seeds and peanuts are two simple ones you can grow yourself, and many people have their own nut trees for

Dried walnuts

a harvest of walnut, hickory nuts, hazelnuts, or pecans. Pumpkin seeds also fall in this category.

Harvesting and acquiring nuts

If you have a source for raw nuts, you certainly can buy them for your own dehydration purposes. Specialty gourmet stores, particularly those that specialize in raw foods, will likely carry them. But the cost of buying such nuts might make the idea of doing your own dehydrating redundant, as it would be cheaper just to buy processed nuts.

Seeds such as sunflower or pumpkin should be much easier to find. Raw varieties usually can be purchased at health food stores or bulk stores that have a selection of nuts and seeds in their inventory.

Otherwise, you will have to grow your own raw nuts. Nut trees might be a bit more of an investment than a casual gardener would want, but you can grow your own sunflower or pumpkin seeds just like "regular" plants. The same goes for peanuts.

When harvesting your own nuts, just remember that they will not necessarily look quite like the nuts you buy in the store because they have not been dried or roasted. Many nuts are harvested once they have fallen from the tree, which makes it easy for you to tell when they are ready.

Preparing nuts and seeds

The biggest preparation step for any nuts or seeds is shelling. Trying to dehydrate nuts while still in the shell is possible but awkward and time-consuming. On the other hand, they do last quite a bit longer in storage if you leave the shells intact. You will have to make that decision based on your nut needs.

Nuts fresh off a tree have an additional layer to them though, usually called a husk. The husk is usually green and will split when the nuts are ready to harvest. The nut and shell you are more familiar with is inside. Just do not confuse the husk with the shell. This applies to tree nuts only.

Peanuts are different than all the others because they grow underground. Once harvested, you will have to give them a quick cleaning.

Other seeds will have their own shells but will need to be harvested in their own way. Sunflower seeds are easy enough to pluck out of a dried flower head, whereas pumpkin seeds will take more effort to get out of a fleshy pumpkin. They should be washed lightly as well. Seeds will have their own shells just like nuts, so you have to decide if you want to shell or not before you dry them. Compared to tree nuts, seeds will dry well even if you leave the shells on.

Methods for drying nuts

Drying nuts and seeds requires a lower temperature than all the other food types so far mentioned, which can make them a little harder to dry if you are not using a true dehydrator. Even with

Sunflower seeds

a dehydrator, it will only work well if you have the type that can be adjusted to a lower temperature. Most nuts and seeds will dry at around 90 F, although specific details are coming later in this section.

The reason is the high oil content in nuts and seeds. Too much heat, and they will start to go rancid. It will not ruin the nuts, considering they are heated during roasting without doing any harm. But it does mean that they will start to spoil much more quickly. Seeds are usually more tolerant of high temperatures than nuts are.

So, you can either use a dehydrator or sun drying for your nuts and seeds. Even a warm room in the house can work as long as the air is moving around somewhat.

Compared to fruits and vegetables, you can dehydrate some seeds and nuts quickly because they really do not have that much moisture in them to begin with. You do not leave these kinds of foods overnight in the dehydrator or several days in the sun.

Storing dried nuts

Even when dried, nuts will not store as long as other dehydrated foods. The fat and oils inside the nuts are just not that shelf-stable and will start to deteriorate even when all the moisture has been removed. On average, nuts with their shells removed will only last about three months when stored at room temperature. Un-shelled nuts will last longer, usually closer to six months. If you have the space, you can store either form of nut in the fridge, and they will last twice as long.

To store them, they need to be in an airtight container and kept away from the light. This applies whether you are storing them in the refrigerator or just on a shelf.

Instructions for drying nuts and seeds

Because roasting nuts is the most common way to prepare them after they have been dried, temperatures for that are being included here. Just remember that drying your nuts removes moisture and improves their shelf life. Roasting is a whole other step that actually cooks the nuts to bring out their flavor. You certainly can use dried nuts without having to roast them if you wish.

Pumpkin Seeds

Once you give them a wash and light scrub to remove all the remaining pumpkin flesh, you are ready to dry your pumpkin seeds. It is not necessary to shell them.

Dehydrator: Set to 115 F, three to four hours.
Sun drying: Six to eight hours in direct sun

Oven: Set to 115 F, four to six hours.

Roasting: 250 F for 15 minutes, still in their shells

Peanuts

Peanuts are different from most other nuts, and they are not as sensitive to high heats. That means you can dehydrate them using more conventional means.

Dehydrator: Set at 130 F, three to four hours.

Sun drying: One day in full sun

Oven: Set at 130 F, four to six hours.

Air drying: One to two weeks in a warm location

Roasting: 350 F for 15 minutes if shelled, closer to 25 if still in the shell

While on the subject of peanuts, you also should know that peanut butter cannot be dehydrated with home equipment. If you were thinking of drying some for storage or for trail snacks, it is not a good idea. The high fat content in peanut butter will keep it from drying out thoroughly, and it will not dehydrate.

Sunflower Seeds

These can be left in the sunflower head to dry almost completely in the sun before you harvest them.

Dehydrator: Set at 100 F, six to eight hours.

Sun drying: One day in full sun

Oven: Set at 100 F, eight to 12 hours.

Roasting: 300 F for 35 to 45 minutes, for seeds in the shell

Tree Nuts

Not all tree nuts are the same, but they generally do dehydrate much the same way so that separate instructions are not necessary. These are some general guidelines to use if you plan to dry walnuts, pecans, hickory nuts, hazelnuts, or any similar type of nut. The shells are harder than with peanuts, so it is better to dry and roast them once they have been shelled.

Dehydrator: Set at 100 F, six to eight hours.
Sun drying: Ten to 14 hours in sunlight or light shade
Oven: Set at 100 F, eight to ten hours.
Air Drying: One to two weeks in a warm area
Roasting: Between 250 F and 300 F for 15 minutes (it will depend on the type of nut)

Coconut

Though not a nut like the others listed and not something that most people are going to grow on their own, being able to dry coconut might come in handy. When buying fresh coconuts at a grocery store, you can use your dehydrator to dry the white flesh for a longer storage time. The best way to dry coconut is to shred the flesh into slivers before dehydrating. For the best taste and texture, you will want to dry it until it is chewy, but it will store better if dried until crisp.

Dehydrator: Set at 115 F, between 24 and 30 hours.
Sun drying: Two to three days in full sun
Oven: Set at 115 F, two to three days.
Roasting: You do not need to roast coconut to bring out the flavor.

Growing your own nuts

Just as with fruit, you can choose from regular garden-growing seeds and nuts, as well as larger trees. All of the seeds mentioned in this chapter are from annual plants you will have to plant each year for a new crop (that includes peanuts). They will need a long growing season, so they might not be suitable for northern re-

gions. However, by starting your seeds indoors, you can grow any of the seed plants mentioned here.

If you are growing sunflowers, you might want to put

Peanut plants

a large paper bag over the flower head once it starts to die and dry to keep the birds from taking off with your seed crop. Pumpkin and peanut plants will not need such protection because their seeds are not exposed.

For growing tree nuts, your options will depend on your climate. Because they have to survive for years, your winter conditions are going to be something to consider. Pecans will not do well in cold winter weather, but walnuts will thrive, for example. *Check your local growing zone on the hardiness map in Chapter 5 to see what nut trees can survive the winters in your area.*

Seeds can be moved around the garden from year to year, but a nut tree is a more permanent addition to your garden space. Take your time researching the tree and choosing the best possible lo-cation. Some trees will get tall and/or wide, so remember that it might start to shade parts of your yard in ten to 20 years.

When it comes to harvesting tree nuts, you are mostly in luck. Many trees actually will drop their nuts when they are ripe, which makes harvesting relatively easy. Crawling on the ground can be easier than trying to pick nuts out of a tall tree. When they do start to drop, you should plan to harvest immediately. Squirrels and many other animals will take advantage of the nuts all over the grass.

Dehydrating Breads

There are only a few instances where you might want to use your dehydrator for bread, but they are worth mentioning. The main use for a dehydrator when it comes to bread products is to make either croutons or dried bread crumbs.

Acquiring and preparing breads

You can use any bread you have on hand at home, usually some that has already started to go stale. That does not mean any bread that shows signs of mold or mildew though. An inexpensive way to get more bread to dry would be the "day old" bread rack at the grocery store or bakery. Because you are doing to dry it anyway, stale or almost-stale bread will work just fine. Homemade bread also works fine.

To prepare for drying, there is little to do. Just tear the pieces of bread into small pieces, or cut more deliberately into cubes if you want that kind of shape for your croutons.

Methods for drying breads

Depending on how dry the bread already is when you begin the dehydration process, you might be able to use any of the typical methods for drying bread. Even just plain air drying will work, though you should watch your bread to make sure mold does not set in while it dries.

The oven and dehydrator work well to dry out bread, though the best results can require higher heat than some dehydrators can muster. In that case, just let them dry longer until the pieces of bread are completely crisp and dry. The sun works quite well for bread as well, but you do need to cover all your trays to keep the birds and pests out.

Storing dried breads

If you make your dried bread products without any additional oils or seasonings, they will store for longer periods. They will last at least six months or longer. When making croutons with oil or herbs, then they might only last two or three months.

Once dried, you should store your bread the same as any other dried food product. A tightly sealed container is best. Light is not quite as big a problem with bread as it is with fruit or vegetables, but it is still best to leave the container in a dark place.

Instructions for drying breads

These instructions will apply for most types of breads or buns you are drying, but the moisture content will vary from one type to another (white versus rye, for example) so you might need to adjust the timing with some practice.

Bread Crumbs

Tear your bread into small pieces for drying, then run the chunks through a blender to make fine dried bread crumbs.

Dehydrator: Set at 140 F, four to six hours.
Sun drying: Six to ten hours in full sun
Oven: Set at 140 F, four to six hours.

Croutons

Cut your pieces of bread into small cubes, and then set to dry. If you want seasoned croutons, add a little garlic, onion, or whatever spice you like before they start drying.

Dehydrator: Set at 140 F, four to six hours.
Sun drying: Six to ten hours in full sun
Oven: Set at 140 F, four to six hours.

Bagel Chips

This is a good way to make a tasty snack out of stale bagels. Slice a bagel into thin round slices (about ¼ inch), and season with whatever flavors you want.

Dehydrator: Set at 140 F, six to eight hours.
Sun drying: Eight to ten in full sun
Oven: Set at 140 F, six to eight hours.

Rising bread dough

While on the subject of bread, you should know that you actually could use your dehydrator to help you while making homemade bread as well. The gentle warm air inside a dehydrator is perfect for helping bread dough rise.

You can really only do this if you have a cabinet-style dehydrator that you can remove the trays from to leave a large open space inside. A dehydrator that is made up of stacked trays will not work. Take out the trays, and set your fresh dough inside with a small bowl of water (you do not want to dry out your bread dough while doing this). Set your dehydrator to 115 F, and your dough should be done rising in less than an hour.

Drying Pasta

This is just a quick note about a further use for your dehydrator to dry home-made fresh pasta. You have to make your pasta as you normally would; this is just for the final step of drying it for longer storage. If you have very long noodles, they may not lay out straight if you have a smaller dehydrator with round trays. So just cut your noodles down to fit if necessary.

Lay out your pasta in the dehydrator, and set to 125 F. Dry for six to eight hours, depending on the thickness and style of your pasta. When done, noodles should be brittle and snap when bent.

Chapter 10

DRYING MEAT AND FISH

Using a dehydrator to dry meat or fish is not as common as using it with fruits and vegetables, mainly because it is more complicated and does have a greater potential for health risks. But once you have some experience drying food at home, there is no reason why you cannot branch out and make some dried fish or meat jerky as well. Fundamentally, drying meat is no different than drying other foods, so the basic ideas you have already learned still will apply.

Special Health Considerations

A few things make drying meat different than drying anything else so far listed in this book (fruit, herbs, grains, vegetables, etc.).

First is the fat content. Meat can have a considerable amount of fat in it, which will go rancid no matter how dry you process it. This  can lead to spoilage and health risks for any dried meat you wish to store for any length of time. To keep this to a minimum, you need to select the leanest pieces of meat you can find and take the time to trim away any visible fat before you start dehydrating.

Second, there is a higher bacterial load present when you are dealing with any kind of meat or fish (compared to plant-based foods). This can lead to food poisoning if your foods are not dried quickly enough or thoroughly enough. The removal of moisture will prohibit any bacterial growth, just like with other foods, but you have to get the right dryness level quickly. With the exception of making jerky, all meats to be dried should be thoroughly cooked first. This will kill any bacteria present in the meat, which will make the drying process much safer.

Although it might be a little riskier than other foods, once it is properly cooked and dried, dehydrated meat can last for several months or up to a year in storage.

Preparing Meat and Fish to Be Dried

There can be more preparation necessary for meat and fish, although drying leftover meat that already has been cooked will make this go quicker. Otherwise, you will have to cook all of your meat before you can start it drying. Details for making jerky with raw meat will be included later because it is more time-consuming, and there are more things to watch out for.

Choosing appropriate meat and fish

You want the leanest meats you can find. Certain meats, such as duck or goose, naturally are going to be too fatty for drying and should be avoided. Each type of meat will have its own criteria for getting the best cuts because every animal is a little different.

Choosing Beef

The best cut of beef for drying is a lean roast, although you can also get a decent dried product if you use extra lean ground beef. Even thinly sliced roast beef from the deli counter will work well.

Choosing Pork

Generally, pork is not great for drying due to its fat content. Cured ham is the only exception. Smoked or cured ham can be dried, although any excess fat should be removed, and the meat should be cooked beforehand. Again, deli meat even could be used. Bacon is also smoked, but the cuts of meat used for bacon have too much fat to store well when dried.

Choosing Poultry

You should avoid trying to dry duck or goose meat because it is too oily to dehydrate safely. Otherwise, you can dry chicken or turkey just fine. White meat pieces will dry the best because of the lower fat content.

Choosing Fish and Seafood

You can use fresh or frozen fish or even dry some canned fish (make sure to drain and rinse first). Any type of fish will work, and you can dry other types of seafood, such as shrimp, in much the same way. For shrimp, you will have to peel and devein before drying. Many people who enjoy dried shrimp use precooked shrimp to speed things up (even those shrimp ring appetizers can be used). Pieces of crab or lobster meat also can be dried.

Choosing Game Meats

During hunting season, there may be more meat available at once than you can handle, so many will turn to dehydration for a quick way to store extra meat. Whether you are a hunter yourself or buy game meat from others, this is another option for drying.

The same rules apply with deer, elk, or moose as they do for the other meats. You need to dry only the leanest meat possible and trim off all the excess fat.

Saving Money Buying Meat

You can use the typical cuts of meat that you normally would buy to cook, and you can save a little money by buying when the grocery store marks the older meat down. You only should do this if you plan on doing your cooking and drying right away, or you run the risk of dealing with spoiled meat before you even get started.

Further savings can be had if you buy in quantity, within reason. Buying a one-fourth of a cow directly from a meatpacking facility might seem like an ideal way to save some money, but you will not be able to choose precisely the cuts you want.

Cleaning and preparing meat for drying

No matter what type of meat you are going to dehydrate, you will want to remove the skin and trim away any visible fat. Once the meat has been properly trimmed, it needs to be thoroughly cooked.

You want to keep your meat tender, so choosing the right method for cooking can make a big difference in the quality of your dried meat later. Most meat will do best when braised or baked, and a pressure cooker can help speed up the process as well as keep the meat tender. Fish should be steamed or poached. Regardless of the method, the meat or fish must be thoroughly cooked through.

Methods for Drying Meat and Fish

You are going to be more limited in your method options for meat and fish because some drying techniques that worked fine for fruit and vegetables are not up to the task of drying meat.

Sun and air drying

Though people have dried meat in the sun for centuries, it is not considered a safe method by today's standards. The temperatures involved are not high enough to dry meat safely, and the irregularity of the temperature levels adds to the risk.

Oven drying meat and fish

Photo courtesy of Douglas and Sherri Brown

The oven is one of the better options for dehydrating meat because the temperature settings are more appropriate. Most meats dry best at 110 F to 150 F, which is within the range of more oven models than the temperatures used for other foods. As with other drying, when drying meat in the oven, you must leave the door partly open due to the higher temperatures.

Dehydrating meat and fish

Using a dehydrator can be difficult depending on your model. Your machine will need to reach temperatures of at least 140 F, which might be a little too high for the simpler models without thermostat control. Unlike other foods that can just be dried longer when the temperature is lower, this is not a safe approach when dehydrating meats. If your machine cannot reach 140 F (or more, ideally 150 F), you either should upgrade to a stronger dehydrator or plan to use the oven for this particular drying project.

Storing Dried Meat

Dried meat can be stored at room temperature in any container with a tight-fitting lid. Keeping it in the fridge can prolong its shelf life, particularly if you are still new at drying meat.

Instructions for Drying Meat and Fish

Be warned that drying meat (especially fish) is extremely aromatic and can be a little disturbing in the house if you are doing other cooking. It might be a good idea to set up your dehydrator in a spare room so you can contain the smells. If nothing else, or if using your oven, plan to open some windows.

Beef

Once thoroughly cooked, cut your beef into small pieces. You will get the evenest drying if you stick with ½-inch cubes. If any droplets of oil start to form on the surface of the meat, blot them off with paper towel. During drying, give the pieces a gentle stirring to help keep them evenly dehydrating. When your beef is fully dry, it will be hard, not leathery.

Dehydrator: Set at 140 F, six to ten hours.

Oven: Set at 140 F, eight to 12 hours.

To rehydrate: Simmer dried beef in equal parts water to beef for at least 50 minutes.

Ham

Only use smoked or cured ham for dehydrating, and it still should be cooked before you dry it. Dice up the cooked ham to ¼-inch pieces for the best results. Check on  your ham while it dries to blot any drops of oil or fat that start to form. Ham is completely dry when the pieces are solid and hard.

Dehydrator: Set at 140 F, five to eight hours.

Oven: Set at 140 F, six to ten hours.

To rehydrate: Simmer one part ham to one part water for about an hour.

Poultry

Remove skin and underlying fat, and then cook your chicken completely. Pressure-cookers are great for doing chicken for dehydrating. Slice up the meat into cubes that are about ½ inch in size. Stir the pieces around during drying to keep the drying uniform.

Dehydrator: Set at 140 F, six to eight hours.

Oven: Set at 140 F, eight to ten hours.

To rehydrate: Simmer in equal parts water for 45 minutes until soft.

Fish

Fish should be cooked, skinned, and then flaked apart for drying. The pieces should be no larger than ¼ inch in thickness. If you are going to use canned fish (such as tuna or salmon), drain it thoroughly, and give it a quick rinse before you set it up in the dehydrator.

Dehydrator: Set at 140 F, three to six hours.
Oven: Set at 140 F, four to eight hours.
To rehydrate: Steam for about 15 to 20 minutes.

Venison

Venison is the proper term for deer meat and is more often used to make jerky than simple dried meat due to the strong flavor. But you certainly can dry it as cooked meat as well. You will want to cut the meat into ½-inch cubes, just like you would when drying beef. In fact, venison is better for drying than beef because it is naturally much leaner.

Dehydrator: Set at 140 F, six to ten hours.
Oven: Set at 140 F, eight to 12 hours.
To rehydrate: Simmer pieces of dried venison in equal parts water for just under an hour.

Shrimp

Your shrimp should be cooked and cleaned (in other words, ready to eat). If they are wet on the outside, give them a good pat with a paper towel to remove any ex-

tra moisture before you begin. When done, properly dehydrated shrimp will be hard.

> *Dehydrator:* Set at 140 F, six to eight hours.
> *Oven:* Set at 140 F, six to ten hours.
> *To rehydrate:* Soak 1 cup of shrimp in ½ cup of hot water until soft. You also can eat dehydrated shrimp as a snack while still dry.

Crabmeat

Because crabmeat is quite expensive, it generally is not used for dehydrated meat. But you can use the cheaper imitation crabmeat (which is made mostly of fish meat) to recreate the taste of crab for dried snacks and meals. These instructions are for imitation meat, but real crabmeat likely would work much the same. Use flaked meat, or cut larger pieces into ¼-inch slices. The pieces should be hard when done, not pliable.

> Dehydrator: Set at 140 F, six to eight hours.
> Oven: Set at 140 F, eight to ten hours.
> To rehydrate: Simmer for about 20 minutes.

Tofu

Though not really a meat, tofu is a popular meat replacement that also can be dehydrated. You can dry it, and it does make a good protein-rich substitute for meat in many camping or trail recipes. Choose the firmest style you can get, and you can make a decent tofu jerky with your dehydrator.

Because tofu holds so much water within to start, you should try to press out as much as possible before starting up the dehydrator. Wrap your chunk of tofu in a layer or two of paper towels, and set a plate on top. Add something like a can of soup on the plate for a little weight, and let the extra water squeeze out for about half an hour.

Once pressed, you can soak your tofu in a marinade (such as soy sauce), for two to three hours. It will soak it up fast; so, it should not need to steep overnight. Then you are ready to dry. Slice each piece to a ¼ inch thickness. When done, it will be tough and leathery. You probably should flip the pieces over after three to four hours.

> *Dehydrator:* Set at 140 F, six to ten hours.
> *Oven:* Set at 140 F, eight to 12 hours.
> *To rehydrate:* Eat dry as a form of jerky, or simmer in water until it softens up.

Recipes using Dried Meat and Fish

Dried meat can be used in many types of dishes that normally would use cooked meat. You even can eat dried meat as a snack, but any meat that has been cooked first will be quite a bit tougher when dried than jerky is. It is better to cook with dried meat and only try to snack on jerky.

Beef and Vegetable Stew

This classic beef stew not only uses your dried meat but also a number of dried vegetables as well. You can use any mix of vegetables that you like to make up the 3 cups. Vegetables that go well with this type of dish include carrots, green beans, peas, celery, mushrooms, turnips, or corn.

- 3 cups water, boiling
- 1 ½ cups dried beef
- 3 cups dried vegetables

- 2 Tbsp. dried onion pieces
- ¼ cup flour
- ¼ cup water

Pour the first measure of boiling water over the dried beef and continue to heat at a simmer for about 45 minutes. Stir in the dried vegetables and onion, and keep simmering for another half an hour. As the stew is getting close to being done, mix the flour and second measure of water in a small bowl until smooth. Slowly stir the flour mixture into the stew pot until everything is combined, and the stew has thickened to your liking. Serve hot, and it will make about six servings.

Beef Stroganoff Noodles

This recipe uses weight for the beef to be more accurate; so get out your kitchen scales. You will get two servings from this recipe.

- 1 oz. dried beef
- ⅓ cup dried mush-
  room pieces
- 1 tsp. dried parsley
- ¼ tsp. paprika
- 1 ½ cups water
- 2 cups noodles or rice
  of your choice
- 4 Tbsp. sour cream
- ¼ cup milk

Mix beef, mushrooms, parsley, and paprika in water and bring to a boil. Reduce the heat to a simmer, and cook for about 20 minutes. Add the noodles and milk, and continue to simmer. When the noodles and beef are soft to your liking, remove from heat, and stir in the sour cream. Serve immediately.

Chicken and Broccoli Casserole

A creamy casserole that cooks up quickly when you use both dried chicken and broccoli as well as canned soup in the sauce.

- 1 cup dried chicken
- 1 cup dried broccoli pieces
- 2 cups water
- 1 can cream of broccoli soup
- 1/3 cup milk
- 1/2 cup Cheddar cheese, grated or shredded
- 3 Tbsp. bread crumbs

Combine dried chicken and broccoli in water, and bring to a simmer. Let it cook for about half an hour until it starts to soften. At that point, start the oven preheating to 450 F. Fill a 9-inch pie pan with the chicken and broccoli mixture. In another bowl, whisk together the soup and milk, and then pour over the chicken and broccoli. Top with bread crumbs and a generous sprinkling of shredded cheese.

Bake for about 20 minutes until the cheese starts to brown on top. Let it sit for another five minutes out of the oven to set, and then serve.

Tuna Casserole

Many tuna casseroles use canned soup for the sauce, but this one is more of a made-from-scratch type of dish.

- ¾ cup dried peas
- ¾ cup dried fish
- 1 ½ cup warm water
- 8 oz. package of noodles
- 2 Tbsp. butter

- 2 Tbsp. flour
- 1 cup milk
- 1 cup shredded cheese

Pour warm water over the peas and fish, and let soak until most of the water has been absorbed, and the food starts to soften. You do not need to have it completely rehydrated, as both the peas and fish will absorb more liquid in the casserole as it bakes. While it is soaking, cook the noodles until they are softer but still firm. Drain out the water.

Start preheating your oven to 350 F, and grease a casserole dish.

In a small cooking pot, heat butter until melted, and stir in the flour until it is smooth. Whisk in the milk and then the shredded cheese. Pour over the noodles, peas, and fish, and then stir to combine. Spoon the mixture into the casserole, and bake for about 35 minutes until the top starts to brown.

Chicken Curry

Many recipes that use dried foods can be bland, but this curry is loaded with spices. It is more complicated than most recipes in this book, so do not plan on this as a quick meal. This recipe will serve two.

- 2 cups dried chicken pieces
- ½ cups water
- 1 Tbsp. olive oil
- ½ red onion, diced
- ½ bay leaf
- 1 tsp. water
- 1 tsp. turmeric

- ⅛ tsp. chili powder
- ⅛ tsp. paprika
- 2 tsp. ginger
- 3 tsp. garlic, minced
- 1 tsp. water
- ½ tomato, diced
- ⅛ tsp. sugar
- 1 cardamom pod, crushed
- 1 whole clove
- 1 small cinnamon stick
- 1 tsp. butter
- 1 Tbsp. water
- 1 tsp. coriander

Start soaking chicken pieces for about 20 minutes before you start the rest of the recipe. Combine oil, onion, and bay leaf, and sauté in a skillet until the onion is soft and starting to brown. Add first teaspoon of water to the pan along with the turmeric, chili, paprika, ginger, and garlic. Reduce heat to a simmer, and cook until it starts to thicken. Then add another teaspoon of water.

Add in the chicken and tomato, and stir through the sauce. Add sugar, cardamom, clove, cinnamon stick, butter, and the last tablespoon of water. Heat on low, with a lid, for about 20 minutes. If the sauce gets too thick or dry, add more water.

Instructions for Making Jerky

Because jerky is different than just drying plain meat, it requires more instructions. Specific seasoning recipes will come later in the next section. This is strictly the how-to information.

Any meat will do, although the best jerky is made with brisket or flank steak. Of course, you can experiment with jerky made with other meats as well, including chicken, turkey, or fish. But basic meat jerky is made with beef or venison. When you are planning your dehydrating, keep in mind that about 3 pounds of meat will dry down to about 16 ounces.

Slice the raw meat into 1/8-inch slices, usually in strips 1 to 2 inches wide (for more convenient travel-sized pieces). The best way to slice raw meat is by freezing it first. Whether you cut with or against the grain seems to be a matter of preference, although slices with the grain are the chewiest. As you slice, remove as much fat as possible.

Once your slices are complete, you have to treat the meat in whatever marinade or spice rub that you want. This part is variable, and there are countless recipes for jerky spices. Depending on the recipe, you might have to leave the meat overnight in the fridge.

When the meat is ready to dry, you can either dry it with a dehydrator or oven but not out in the sun. It is no longer considered safe, and you run the risk of bacterial contamination if the temperature is not high enough. Your dehydrator will have to be able to reach 140 F for this to work. Otherwise, do your jerky drying in the oven just like other dried meat. Do not mix any other drying in with it unless it is other meat.

Lay your seasoned strips of meat out on your oven or dehydrator trays, and dry at 140 F for six hours. Then flip all the pieces over, and continue drying for another six hours. When properly dried, your jerky should be tough and brittle.

Ground meat jerky

Though it is not as traditional, you can also use ground meats to make jerky. The recipes for this type of jerky usually blend the ingredients together with the meat rather than soaking the meat in a marinade. Ground meat jerkies are not as chewy as the strip meat variety.

It is best to use a recipe intended for ground meat because most other marinades are too much of a liquid, as they are intended to use as a soak for meat.

To make jerky this way, blend the ground meat (beef or otherwise) according to the recipe, and then use a jerky gun or a pastry bag to create thin strips of meat mixture. Just fill the bag with meat, and squeeze out the mix through the tip of the bag. Even a large zip-close bag with one corner snipped off might work if the bag is sturdy enough. Another way is to just spread a thin layer like you are making a fruit leather and let it dry that way.

Set your oven or dehydrator at 140 F and dry for about six hours before flipping all the pieces of jerky over. They dry for at least another four to six hours until it is dried hard and tough.

Because you are using raw meat for making jerky (strip meat or ground meat), your dehydrator trays must be well cleaned afterward before you put any other food back on them. In fact, all your cutting surfaces and utensils must be washed and not used for any other dehydrating until they are cleaned.

Recipes for Jerky

These are marinade and spice mixes for making jerky, not recipes that actually *use* jerky. Jerky usually is eaten as is for a dried snack while hiking. But if you have jerky on hand, you can substitute these flavored dried meats for the meat in the above recipes.

Cajun Jerky

This mix of spices works for 1 pound of raw meat, usually beef.

- 4 tsp. brown sugar
- 2 Tbsp. paprika
- 2 tsp. salt
- 2 tsp. dry mustard powder
- ½ tsp. ground ginger powder
- ¼ tsp. allspice powder
- ¼ tsp. cayenne pepper

Combine, and use to coat strips of raw meat. Let steep overnight in the fridge before starting your dehydrating.

Smoked Turkey Jerky

Intended for turkey, you can use this smoky blend with any poultry. It is for 1 pound of meat.

- ¼ cup BBQ sauce
- ½ Tbsp. liquid smoke
- ¼ tsp. chili powder
- ¼ Tbsp. Worcestershire sauce
- Pinch of cayenne (more if you want the heat)

Stir ingredients together until well mixed, and soak meat strips overnight before drying. If you are not familiar with "liquid smoke," you can purchase small bottles of this seasoning where you normally would get BBQ sauces and other grilling condiments. It adds a unique smoky flavor.

Sweet and Spicy Tropical Jerky

You can use this marinade for any meat (for one pound) you wish.

- 1 tsp. salt
- 1 Tbsp. brown sugar
- 1 tsp. ground ginger
- ¼ tsp. black pepper
- ⅛ tsp. cayenne pepper
- 1 garlic clove, crushed or minced fine
- ¼ cup pineapple juice
- ¼ cup soy sauce

Mix the wet and dry ingredients together, and whisk until everything is dissolved and blended. Soak your meat strips for at least a few hours, or better, overnight. Then dehydrate in your preferred method.

Teriyaki Jerky

This one is nicely spiced but also has a citrus touch of orange juice. You need 1 pound of meat, and it goes best with beef. It is more complicated than the other marinades, but the complex flavors are worth it.

- 1 tsp. onion powder
- ½ tsp. garlic powder
- 1 Tbsp. brown sugar
- 2 tsp. salt
- ¼ tsp. ground black pepper
- ⅔ cup teriyaki sauce
- ½ cup orange juice
- ¼ cup water
- 1 tsp. soy sauce
- 1 tsp. liquid smoke

- 1 Tbsp. liquid honey

Whisk everything together until the sugar is dissolved and the whole thing is nicely blended. Soak your meat overnight, and then dehydrate.

Hot Chili Jerky

Another classic jerky blend, but a little heavier on the hot chili side.

- ½ cup soy sauce
- ½ cup Worcestershire sauce
- ¼ cup brown sugar
- 3 cloves minced garlic
- 2 tsp. ground black pepper
- 2 tsp. ground red chili
- 1 tsp. onion powder

Whisk together and soak your meat strips for at least an hour, but overnight is a little too long. Dry as you normally do for jerky.

Curried Jerky

This spicy recipe for jerky has a different flavor from the usual chili peppers. This mixture will be enough for 1 pound of raw meat.

- 1 tsp. salt
- ¼ tsp. coarse black pepper
- ⅛ tsp. ground cinnamon
- 1/16 tsp. ground cloves
- ⅛ tsp. ground cumin
- 2 tsp. curry powder
- ½ tsp. garlic powder
- 1 tsp. ground ginger powder

Blend all the ingredients together, and toss with meat to give it a good coating. Let it sit in the fridge overnight before drying.

BBQ Jerky

Another classic jerky recipe that has the sweet and spicy taste of BBQ will suit any type of meat. Use this mix to marinade 1 pound of sliced raw meat.

- 1 tsp. salt
- ¼ tsp. black pepper
- ⅛ tsp. cayenne
- 1 tsp. garlic powder
- 1 tsp. onion powder
- 1 tsp. dry mustard
- 3 Tbsp. brown sugar
- ⅓ cup red wine vinegar
- ⅓ cup ketchup

Stir everything together until the sugar is dissolved. Soak your meat for at least six hours or overnight is better. Then dehydrate.

Peppercorn Jerky

This is a recipe for making ground beef jerky with the spices mixed into the meat mixture before drying.

- 1 lb. ground beef
- ½ cup minced onion
- 6 cloves of minced garlic
- 2 tsp. salt
- 2 tsp. coarse black pepper (not whole peppercorns though)

Mix everything together except for teaspoon of pepper. Work the meat mixture by hand or in a food processor until all the ingredients are smoothly blended, and the meat is like a thick paste.

Make into strips for dehydrating, and sprinkle the remaining teaspoon of pepper on the outside. You do not need to let the mixture sit or marinate.

Herby Jerky

This is also a ground beef jerky recipe, although the blend is mild enough to mix with any kind of ground meat, not just beef. You can use dried herbs for this if you wish, but you should rehydrate them first because there is not enough moisture in the recipe to compensate.

- 1 lb. ground beef
- ½ cup minced onion
- 4 cloves of minced garlic
- 1 cup fresh parsley
- 1 Tbsp. fresh oregano
- 1 Tbsp. fresh sage
- 2 tsp. salt
- ½ tsp. black pepper

Combine all the ingredients together, and blend by hand or food processor to make a heavy paste. Then use your preferred method to make strips for dehydrating, and dry right away.

Hot Venison Jerky

This recipe is quite hot and goes very well with game meats such as venison. You can use this mix with any kind of meat though. It is a larger recipe than the others — for 3 lbs. of whatever ground meat you choose.

- 3 lbs. ground venison or other meat
- 1 Tbsp. salt
- ¼ cup red wine

- 1 Tbsp. cider vinegar
- 2 tsp. black pepper
- 1 tsp. chili powder
- 1 tsp red pepper flakes

Combine, and mix thoroughly in a food processor until somewhat smooth. Form into strips and dry.

CASE STUDY: STARTING OFF STRONG

Silvia Harvey
Arab, AL 35016 USA
www.happypawshaven.org

Silvia is a relative novice at dehydrating compared to the other case studies. She has been at it for about three years now and is currently doing her drying with a 9-tray Excalibur dehydrator. She has pretty much done it all already. Over these few years, she has dehydrated meat, fish, shrimp, chicken, nuts, vegetables, and many different kinds of fruit. Silvia has yet to come across any foods that give her any trouble. In particular, she finds that she dries ingredients for soup and stew mixes, spice mixes, homemade pasta, and homemade fruit leather the most often. She even uses her dehydrator to make cat and dog treats.

Her standard preparation for drying includes a spritzing of lemon juice to keep fruit from going brown, and some vegetables (such as the root crops) are blanched. Aside from spritzing with lemon juice, she recommends that you do all your slicing carefully, so that everything dries evenly.

Another important tip that she has is that you should always adjust your drying time if the weather is humid. It can take quite a lot longer when the air is already moist. And do not dry onions or garlic indoors.

Silvia stores her dried goods in heavy-duty vacuum bags with a small packet that clears out the oxygen. Some pantry items are kept in glass Mason jars, also with an oxygen pack.

DRYING DAIRY PRODUCTS

Using a dehydrator to dry milk, cheese, or other dairy products is not the most common practice at home, but it certainly can be done with good results. Just keep in mind that this is not a chapter for the dehydrator novice. But once you know the right techniques, you can expand your drying projects to include these foods as well. Being able to store a little milk, cheese, or eggs for an emergency is not a bad idea, and for some recipes, dried milk, cheese, or egg powder is the easiest way to add a bit of flavor or make a sauce. The forms of dairy covered are milk, cheeses, yogurt, and eggs. Butter is not something you can safely dry at home due to its fat content.

Special Health Considerations

Just like with meat, you need to be aware of a few extra issues when thinking about doing any dairy dehydrating. For dairy, the main problem is also the fat content. Fat will go rancid after a relatively short time, which makes any dairy product a risky proposition for long-term storage.

Because of this, you should choose the lowest fat content of whatever you are drying (milk, cheese, etc). The same goes for yogurt, but the acid content helps preserve it after dehydration.

When using your own "home grown" milk, you still will want to remove as much fat as possible before doing any dehydrating. This means you should let the milk settle and then skim the heavy cream that comes to the top. After sitting overnight in the fridge, you can remove most of the cream with a large spoon or ladle. Goat's milk is not a good option for dehydration because it has a high fat content, and that fat cannot be removed like it can with cow's milk. The cream layer will not separate out.

Drying Yogurt

Yogurt is great dairy product that can be dried successfully. In fact, it is probably the best one to start with if you are drying dairy for the first time. It works quite a bit like doing leather. *Look back at Chapter 7 for more information about leathers.* Yogurt can be dried as a way of preserving it, but the more typical use is as a tasty dried snack that is eaten like dried fruit or fruit leather. You even can mix yogurt with fruit purée for another leather variety altogether.

You can use these same instructions for drying sour cream, which has the same consistency as yogurt. The only difference will be how you use it (see the end of this section for that).

Preparing yogurt to be dried

Most yogurts will dry just fine, but those with chunks of fruit in them will dry inconsistently. You either can run them through a blender to smooth out the fruit or just buy yogurt that does not have the pieces of fruit.

Prepare your dehydrator by lining the trays with wax paper (you also can line baking pans with wax paper if you are using the oven). A little nonstick spray on the paper might help you peel the dried yogurt off when it is finished.

Methods for drying yogurt

You only should use your oven or dehydrator when drying yogurt. Air drying is not acceptable, and sun drying usually is not consistent enough to be safe for the same reasons as other dairy products.

Storing dried yogurt

The simplest way to store dried yogurt is by leaving it on its wax paper base and just rolling it up. Tuck in the ends and then store these tubes in a cool, dark place. You should not need to refrigerate it.

Specific instructions for drying yogurt

Spread yogurt over the wax paper sheets thinly, no thicker than 1/8 of an inch. A rubber spatula can be helpful for this task. It will be leathery when it has finished drying, although some varieties of yogurt might be a little sticky.

Dehydrator: Set at 125 F, six to eight hours.

Oven: Set at 125 F, eight to ten hours.

Dried yogurt will not rehydrate back to its original liquid form, but it is tasty to eat as a healthy snack in the dry state. That is how most people use it.

 You do not necessarily have to dry yogurt thin in a sheet. Dropping small dollops of yogurt onto your leather sheets or waxed paper can create larger pieces of dried yogurt that could then be added to cereal or trail mix. They will take longer to dry than a sheet of leather, at least another six to eight hours, though it will depend on how thick you make the drops. If adding fruit purée to your yogurt, you will have to extend the drying time by at least four more hours. When creating new mixes, always keep an eye on the drying to get the timing just right.

If you are drying sour cream, you probably will not be eating it dry as a snack. Let it dry until it is hard, and then break it up into a powder form. You then can use it as an addition to sauces or soups, but it will not rehydrate back into a smooth cream to be used on its own.

Making yogurt in a dehydrator

Above has been a discussion on how to dry yogurt, but you actually can make your own yogurt from milk with a dehydrator. The catch for this project is that you only can use the type of dehydrator that has a cabinet with removable trays. You are going to have to put jars of milk inside, so you cannot do that with a dehydrator that is just a stack of loose trays with a lid on top. It also needs to be a machine with a thermostat so you can set it precisely.

There are two ways to make yogurt. Actually, the techniques are the same, but the ingredients differ. You will need bacteria to culture yogurt properly, and you either can buy yogurt starter for this or use finished yogurt. The starter is usually the best choice for a novice because it always will have live culture in it. Using existing yogurt is a little chancier, as you can never tell just what the bacteria population is going to be.

Start with 1 quart of milk. Whole milk will result in a creamier yogurt, but you can choose any type of milk. To get a thicker yogurt, mix in about 1/3 cup of dry milk powder. Heat milk with a double boiler until it reaches 180 F. Accuracy is important in this, so you should have a thermometer ready.

Once it reaches 180 F, take it from the heat and let it cool. A cold-water bath will cool it faster (place your container of hot milk inside a larger bowl with cold water; do not add cold water to the milk). You also could leave it at room temperature if you prefer. Once it cools to 115 F, you are ready to begin.

Stir in ¼ cup of yogurt or 2 tablespoons of commercial starter, and then pour the mixture into clean containers. You either can make one large batch in a jar or pour your mix into smaller cups for single-serve use. Now, get your dehydrator going at

> 115 to 120 F, and set the containers inside. Let it run for about six to eight hours or until it gets to the thickness and flavor you want. You can stir in fruit and sweetener once it is finished to customize your homemade yogurt. It will need to be stored in the fridge.

Dehydrating Milk

Of all the foods mentioned in this book so far, this is the first true liquid mentioned, which means the instructions are going to be a little different. Before trying to dry milk, you should consider other methods of preservation that may be more suitable. Milk does freeze well, although if you need a shelf-stable option, then drying might be your only choice.

Preparing milk for drying

Any milk can be used for drying, but it first must be pasteurized in order to reduce the amount of bacteria present. Nonpasteurized milk (also known as raw milk) should not be used for any dehydrating purposes. Milk purchased from a store is going to be pasteurized, so this is only an issue if you have a source of fresh milk, such as from a local farmer.

For the best results, try to use skim milk. The less fat, the better your dried milk will store. Just like with meat, the fat will quickly go rancid.

Methods for drying milk

When drying milk, you will have to limit your methods to either the oven or a dehydrator. And the stove is not really the best option, but it will do if that is what you have to work with.

Sun drying is not acceptable for drying milk because it takes too long, and there is almost no way to avoid bacterial contamination. You never should dry your milk in the sun.

Storing dried milk

Home-dried milk will not store as long as commercially dried milk, so do not plan to package and store it for a year.

Air (or more accurately, oxygen) is the problem with dried milk just as much as moisture. You can store your dried milk in jars, but storing the powder away from air is even better. Heavy plastic bags and a vacuum sealing unit are ideal for this purpose. Whatever the container, make sure to store away from moisture and sunlight.

Specific instructions for drying milk

Due to the liquid nature of milk, you will have to adjust your drying techniques somewhat. The best approach is to line your dehydrator trays (or oven baking sheets) with wax paper first. Pour just a thin layer of milk onto each tray; try to keep a depth of no more than one-eighth of an inch. If you have a dehydrator that uses slanted or otherwise not flat trays, you might not be able to dry any liquids at all. In that case, try the oven.

Dehydrator: Set at 130 F, 24 to 30 hours.
Oven: Set at 130 F, 26 to 32 hours.

Once it has dried, milk should flake away from the trays and should be ground down further in a blender to make a powder.

To use your dried milk powder, you will want to mix about 1 part milk powder to 2 parts water (so ⅓ cup of powder and ⅔ cup of water to make 1 full cup of milk). You will want to whisk it thoroughly or even run it through a blender to make sure all the powder dissolves properly. It will not reconstitute as easily as store-bought dried milk.

Your dried milk might not be that appealing as a glass of milk to drink, but it can be used nicely in baking or other cooking purposes. When baking with dried milk powder, you can add the powder into the dry ingredients and add the corresponding extra water to the liquid. You do not need to actually remake your milk before adding to the recipe. *You can find recipes that use dried milk at the end of this chapter.*

Dehydrating Cheese

After thinking about drying milk, you will be happy to know that cheese generally works out quite a bit better. Most varieties of cheese can be dried, but the easiest are hard cheeses (such as Cheddar). However, if you need to, you also can dry cottage cheese, though the applications for it are a little more limited.

Preparing cheese for drying

The best approach for drying hard cheese is to grate it first. Larger pieces will not dry thoroughly. Because the oils will come out of the cheese when it starts to heat up, you will need to line your trays with paper towels. More should be on hand because you will need to replace them a few times while your cheese is drying.

You can use most types of hard cheese, but getting older varieties can work better. They have more flavor and naturally less moisture to begin with.

For cottage cheese, choose a low-fat variety. It will keep better, and there will be a lower chance of it going bad in storage.

Methods for drying cheese

Again, you should stick to either the oven or dehydrator for drying cheese. Air drying might work if you have a warm enough area with good ventilation, but it is a little too risky to be recommended here.

With other drying practices, you can sometimes raise the temperature if you want to speed things up. If you try that with cheese, you need to be careful that you do not raise the heat enough to cause your cheese to melt. That will make a huge mess, particularly if it is inside your dehydrator.

If your oven will not lower enough to keep the cheese from melting, you can still try it. Just use wax paper on your trays. The cheese will melt and then dry from there.

Storing dried cheese

Once your shredded cheese is hard and brittle, you can either store it in that form or run it through the food processor to make your own cheese power. Because dried cheese does not rehydrate well, it makes more sense to store it as a powder. Cottage cheese really will not powderize; so, you can store it in small broken-up pieces.

Kept in an airtight container, your dried hard cheese (powdered or in pieces) should last several months. Cottage cheese will not last as long: about two to three weeks at room temperature or a month or two in the fridge. It is not great for long-term food storage but excellent as an immediate use food item (such as for a hiking trip).

Specific instructions for drying cheese

Hard Cheese

As mentioned above, you should lay your shredded cheese out on paper towel to absorb the oil. How often you need to do this is going to depend on your own judgment. Once you see significant oily spots appearing, replace the paper.

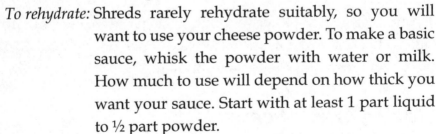

Dehydrator: Set at 120 F, six to eight hours.

Oven: Set at 120 F, eight to ten hours.

To rehydrate: Shreds rarely rehydrate suitably, so you will want to use your cheese powder. To make a basic sauce, whisk the powder with water or milk. How much to use will depend on how thick you want your sauce. Start with at least 1 part liquid to ½ part powder.

Cottage Cheese or Ricotta

Line your trays or pans with wax paper, and spread a thin layer of cheese. When it is done, the pieces will be brittle.

Dehydrator: Set at 130 F, six to eight hours.

Oven: Set at 130 F, ten to 12 hours.

To rehydrate: On its own, dried cottage cheese will not soften up to be just like the fresh version. But you can simmer it in water (or just let it soak at room temperature) until it has rehydrated, and then mix it in with other sauces. Adding it to tomato sauce for a pasta dish works well.

Drying Eggs

Although eggs are not actually dairy products, they should be mentioned, and they fit better in this chapter than in with the meats.

Preparing eggs for drying

You should not try to dry raw eggs. Before you start any dehydrating, you should cook them first. Giving them a quick whisk and cooking them as scrambled eggs is the easiest and most efficient way of doing this. Bacteria will be killed off, and you have an easier product to work with as you dry.

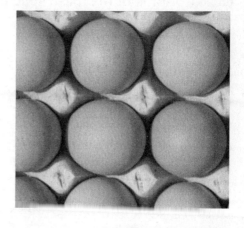

When you cook them, do not add any butter or oil. This added fat would put your dried eggs more at risk for going rancid quickly.

You also can separate your eggs before cooking if you prefer to have only dried egg whites. They can be cooked or used in baking to keep the cholesterol levels down. The overall process will be the same when you dehydrate them.

Methods for drying eggs

As with the other products, this is something that should be done only with the stove or an electric dehydrator. Drying in the sun is too irregular and offers too many potential risks for contamination. In fact, you might find that this is one case where using the oven might be better than the dehydrator.

Eggs should be dried at a higher temperature than most other foods in order to get the moisture fully out in a short period. If your dehydrator can reach 145 F, you can use it. If not, you should try drying in the oven this time.

You should be fine using your standard dehydrator trays for drying scrambled eggs, but some of the pieces will get small and can fall through. Line each tray with a piece of cheesecloth to help close up some of the mesh spacing.

Storing dried eggs

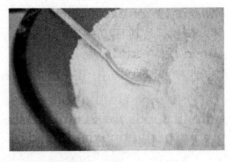

Once dry, you should run the pieces through a blender and store as a powder. Keep your egg powder in an airtight container and in a dark location if using a glass jar. They should store for several months without any problem, but unless you have done egg dehydrating before, you should probably try to use them sooner.

Specific instructions for drying eggs

Dehydrator: Set at 145 F, 16 to 20 hours.
Oven: Set at 145 F, 18 to 24 hours.

To rehydrate: You should be able to use your dried eggs in any way that would normally take eggs. That includes baking as well as actually cooking eggs. Dried eggs can be rehydrated with an equal volume of water, and 1 tablespoon of powder will make about one egg. Once rehydrated, they can be eaten like regular scrambled eggs. If you are using the eggs in baking, you can just add the powdered egg and water to the mix without necessarily rehydrating the egg alone first.

Recipes for Dried Dairy

Because dried dairy products are a little less common around the kitchen, here are a few basic recipes to get you started in using them.

Basic Creamy Cheese Sauce

You can make this at home or mix up the ingredients to use while hiking because everything in it is dehydrated. The mix can be made up ahead of time, so you would just need to add water when you are ready for the sauce.

- ⅓ cup cheese powder
- 3 Tbsp. dried milk powder
- 3 Tbsp. flour
- ¼ tsp. salt
- ⅛ tsp. ground pepper
- ⅛ tsp. onion powder

Stir everything together until the powders are all well blended. You can either store the mix in a tight container or make the sauce right away. You will need about 1 cup of hot water to ½ cup of cheese powder mix (this can be adjusted depending on your taste for a thicker or thinner sauce). Whisk over low heat until it has been simmering for a few minutes. When it is properly blended to the desired thickness, serve over pasta, vegetables, or whatever you wish.

Fruit Smoothie

Some dry milk powder can give you a completely new taste in a smoothie.

- 3 cups fresh fruit
- 1 cup dried milk powder
- ½ cup water
- ½ cup crushed ice
- 1 tsp. vanilla
- 1 Tbsp. sugar

Combine everything in a blender, and blend until smooth. Add a little extra water if it is too thick for your liking.

Most uses for dried milk and other dairy products are associated with dry mixes or trail food mixes rather than cooking in the kitchen. *You can find more of these types of recipes in Chapter 12.*

Mayonnaise with Powdered Egg

Many people avoid making their own mayo because they are not comfortable with raw eggs. By using dried egg powder, you can make mayonnaise more safely at home.

- 1 rounded Tbsp. dried egg powder
- 1 Tbsp. water

- ½ tsp. salt
- 1 Tbsp. lemon juice
- ½ tsp. Dijon mustard
- ½ cup vegetable or olive oil (you might need more)

Combine everything except for the oil in your blender or food processor, and blend until smooth. This is where some patience comes in. You have to add the oil about one teaspoon at a time, and blend well between each addition of oil. This is a little imprecise at this point, but you will want to add enough oil to give the texture and thickness you want with mayonnaise. A half cup is usually enough, but more oil will create a thicker mix.

Swedish Pancakes

Here is one recipe that includes both dried eggs as well as dried milk. This will make a batch of fluffy pancakes, and you could add small pieces of dried fruit as well.

- 3 Tbsp. dried egg powder
- 6 Tbsp. water
- 1 cup dried milk powder
- 3 cups warm water
- 4 Tbsp. butter, melted
- 2 Tbsp. sugar
- 1 tsp. salt
- 1 ½ cups flour

Whisk first measure of water and egg powder together until it is smooth and blended. Stir in the remaining ingredients, adding the flour last. Stir thoroughly until you have a smooth batter. Let it rest for five minutes, and then stir again before making your pancakes.

Cook about ½ cup of batter on a hot skillet or griddle, just like regular pancakes. Flip them over when the edges start to brown in order to cook both sides. Serve hot with syrup or other desired toppings.

Chapter 12

DRIED FOOD RECIPES AND MIXES

There have been recipes all through this book already primarily showing you how to incorporate dried food into your everyday cooking. This chapter is a little different. These mixes are made up mostly of dried foods and usually can be made up before you need them. These include handy mixes for quicker cooking at home as well as dried foods you can take on the trail. Although these mixes are made entirely from dried ingredients, they may not be all foods you are willing to dry yourself (such as some spices, dried meat, or milk powder).

Soup Mixes

Dried foods go well in soup mixes because they are naturally simmered during cooking, so they can rehydrate without any special steps. Many of these recipes have dried beans, which are easy to purchase already dried. Whether you use your home-dried beans, these mixes can create a whole host of soup choices in the kitchen.

In most cases, you will want to store the spice blends apart from the beans or pasta until you are ready to make soup. The easiest way to do this is to keep the spices in a zip-close plastic bag, tucked into a larger jar with the bean mixes.

Five-Bean Winter Soup

You can mix the proportions of beans to suit your own taste as long as you end up with about 5 cups of dried beans.

- 1 cup each of dried pinto beans, lima beans, garbanzo beans
- 2 cups dried kidney beans
- ½ cup dried onion pieces
- 1 Tbsp. paprika
- 2 tsp. salt
- 1 tsp. dried mustard
- ½ tsp. garlic powder
- 4 cubes beef bouillon
- ¼ cup dried bacon bits
- ¼ cup dried vegetable pieces

You can mix the beans together in one container and then the spices in another. Do not combine them until it is time to make your soup. To make six bowls of soup, you should measure out 1 ½ cups of bean mixture along with 5 cups water in a large soup pot. Then stir in ¼ cup of the seasoning mix. Bring it all to a boil, and let it simmer for at least two hours or until the beans are soft and cooked.

Old-Fashioned Bean and Barley Soup

This recipe includes a mix of pasta and rice for a little more starch than the bean-filled one above. It is filling and makes a full meal by itself.

- ½ cup dried barley
- ½ cup dried split peas
- ½ cup uncooked white rice
- ½ cup dried lentils
- 2 Tbsp. dried onion pieces
- 2 Tbsp. dried parsley
- 2 tsp. salt
- ¼ tsp. pepper
- 2 cubes beef bouillon
- 1 ½ cups dry macaroni pasta
- 1 cup dried vegetables, mixed

Combine all the beans, rice, and pasta, and then blend the spices in another container. To make all of this into soup, use 3 quarts of water, and simmer all of the ingredients for an hour. It will make about four servings.

Chicken Noodle Soup

You can make this soup without the chicken meat if you want to keep it an "all dry" mix, but the added meat does make it a heartier soup.

- ¼ cup dried lentils
- 2 Tbsp. dried onion pieces
- 2 cubes chicken bouillon
- ½ tsp. dried dill
- ⅛ tsp. dried celery seed
- ⅛ tsp. dried garlic powder

- 1 bay leaf
- 1 cup dried noodles
- ¾ cup dried vegetable pieces
- 2 cups cooked chicken meat

Like with the other soups, you can mix the spices together in a small bag or container and store along with the lentils and noodles. To make soup, combine everything with 8 cups of water. Bring to a boil, and then turn the heat down to simmer. Cook until everything is tender, and then add the meat. Continue to simmer until the meat has warmed up.

Cream of Broccoli Soup

You can even make cream soups as a dry mix, as long as you have milk powder around.

- 2 cups dried broccoli pieces
- ½ cup dried onion
- ½ cup dried celery
- ½ cup dried milk powder
- 1 Tbsp. dried parsley
- Salt and pepper to taste

With this recipe, you can mix everything together and store it combined until you are ready to make a pot of soup. You need 3 quarts of water for the entire batch of mix. Simmer for about an hour or until the broccoli has softened completely.

Minestrone

A classic soup mix with tomatoes, beans, and pasta. If you have fresh cheese around when you make it, you can sprinkle some over each bowl.

- 1 cup dried tomato pieces
- ¼ cup dried celery
- ¼ cup dried onion
- ¼ cup dried green beans
- ¼ cup dried kidney beans
- ¼ cup dried navy beans
- 1 tsp. dried garlic, minced
- ¼ cup pasta shells

You can combine and store everything together for this recipe, and then use 8 cups of water or your favorite stock to cook it. Just let everything simmer until it is soft and tender.

Potato Soup

This simple soup is made from potatoes. It makes a good base to add additional vegetables or even meat to customize it to your taste. If you have white pepper, it blends better with this pale soup than black pepper does.

- 1 ¾ cup instant mashed potato flakes
- 1 ½ cup dried milk powder
- 2 Tbsp. chicken bouillon powder
- 1 Tbsp. dried onion pieces
- 1 tsp. dried parsley
- ¼ tsp. pepper
- ¼ tsp. dried thyme
- 2 tsp. seasoned salt

Stir everything together, and store in a tight container like a glass jar. To make soup, mix ½ cup of soup mix with 1 cup of boiling water. Stir until it is smooth and ready to eat.

Lentil and Mushroom Soup

There is no meat in this recipe, but the mushrooms add a nice touch "meaty" touch. Rather than water, you will need to have broth on hand to make this soup.

- ¼ cup dried lentils
- ¼ cup dried mushroom pieces (any variety)
- ¼ cup long grain rice
- ¼ cup pearl barley
- ¼ cup split peas
- ½ tsp. celery salt
- ¼ tsp. onion powder
- ¼ tsp garlic powder

This mix should be stored in an airtight container until you are ready to make it. Use the entire contents along with 7 cups of chicken broth. Heat up to a boil, then turn the heat down to keep it simmering. Cook for about 45 to 55 minutes until everything is tender.

Chili

Preparing this mix ahead of time will save you quite a bit of time, but be aware that several wet ingredients will need to be added when it is time to make the chili. Unlike the soups listed so far, this is not a complete recipe in a mix.

- ¼ cup dried parsley
- 2 Tbsp. dried garlic
- 2 Tbsp. taco seasoning
- 1 Tbsp. dried onion pieces
- 1 Tbsp. cumin
- 1 Tbsp. paprika
- 1 Tbsp. cornmeal
- 1 Tbsp. chili powder
- ¼ cup dried navy beans

- ¼ cup dried black beans
- ½ cup dried kidney beans
- 1 cup dried tomato pieces

That makes the dry mix portion. You can store these ingredients mixed together in a closed container or jar.

To make the chili, you will need:

- 1 small onion, diced
- ½ can of tomato paste
- ¼ cup cider vinegar
- ¼ cup brown sugar
- 20 oz. tomato juice
- 1 lb. ground beef

Combine the dry mix with the wet ingredients, and add enough water to cover everything. Bring it to a simmer, and let it cook for between two and three hours. When the beans are tender, you are ready to serve.

Trail Mixes

This section is for all kinds of "trail food" that you can use when hiking or camping. Dry snacks as well as more complicated meals you have to rehydrate or cook when it is time to eat are listed here.

Dry snacks

You usually can eat these dry mixes as a snack while outdoors. They do not require any cooking or preparation. Just mix, store, and later enjoy. Of course, any type of mixture will do. You can create an infinite number of combinations with different kinds of nuts, dried fruit, and other similar ingredients. But a few good recipes can help get your own creativity going.

Basic Fruit and Nut Mix

For a healthy mix on the trail, use un-
salted nuts in this recipe. You will get
4 cups of mix.

- 1 cup of larger dried fruit, such
  as apples, pears, or apricots
- ½ cup smaller dried fruit, such as raisins or cherries
- 1 ½ cups sunflower seeds
- 1 cup roasted peanuts

Sweet Treats Mix

This may not be the healthiest mix, but it does go over well with
kids. There are about 5 cups of mix in this combination.

- 1 cup miniature marshmallows
- ½ cup dried pineapple pieces
- 1 cup dried apricots, chopped
- 1 cup mixed nuts
- ½ cup raisins
- ¼ cup sunflower seeds
- ¾ cup M&Ms (peanut or regular)

Tropical Mix

With a little addition of less-common fruit, you can make a whole
other style of mix.

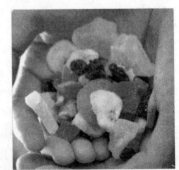

- 1 cup mixed nuts
- ¼ cup sunflower seeds
- ½ cup dried pineapple
- ½ cup dried mango
- ½ cup raisins
- ½ cup dried shredded coconut
- ½ cup dried banana chips

Fruit Snack Clusters

Not all trail mix has to be a loose blend in a bag. These clusters work great for hiking as well as anytime snacking at home.

- ½ cup dried apricots
- ½ cup dried apples
- ½ cup dried peaches
- ½ cup shredded coconut
- ¼ cup almond slivers
- 1 tsp. dry lemon zest
- ½ tsp. cinnamon
- 3 Tbsp. honey
- 3 Tbsp. orange juice
- 1 Tbsp. lemon juice

Dice up all the dried fruit in to small pieces, or run quickly in a food processor. Then stir together all the fruit with coconut, almonds, zest, and cinnamon. In another cooking pot, melt honey with orange and lemon juice until it is all dissolved.

Pour the liquid over the fruit mixture, and combine with your hands until everything is sticky. Form into snack-sized balls and lay out on a leather sheet or wax paper in your dehydrator. Dry for about six hours until they are not sticky on the outside any longer.

Baked Granola Mix

Baking this mixture in the oven before packing for the trail gives this mixture a nice roasted flavor.

- ¼ cup butter
- ⅓ cup brown sugar
- 2 ½ cups raw rolled oats
- ¼ cup almond slivers

- ¼ cup chopped walnuts, pecans, or peanuts
- ½ cup raisins
- ⅓ cup dry dates, chopped
- ⅓ cup dry apricots, chopped
- ⅓ cup dry pears, chopped
- ¼ cup chocolate chips

Preheat your oven to 350 F.

Melt butter, and mix with brown sugar in a small bowl until it is all dissolved. In a larger bowl, mix oats, almonds, and other nuts. When the dry ingredients are nicely coated, spread out on a baking sheet. Bake for 12 minutes until golden brown. Stir at least once part way through. When it is finished, let it cool completely. Break up any large pieces that have stuck together, and then mix with the remaining ingredients. Because of the butter, this mix will not last as long as some of the others.

Cooked mixes for the trail

These mixes are intended to be soaked, simmered, or otherwise prepared before you sit down to eat. Some are just a mix of dry ingredients that can be put together in just a few minutes, but some recipes need to be cooked *before* they are dehydrated. These meals will involve more preparation while still in the kitchen.

Banana Oatmeal

You can have a hot breakfast that will keep you going until lunch. You need to use dried cooked whole oats or quick-cooking oats for this recipe to work with the timing provided. Buying dried oats will probably work best.

- ½ cup dried cooked whole oats, chopped
- ¼ cup dried banana slices
- 2 Tbsp. dry milk powder

- 1 Tbsp. brown sugar
- A pinch of ground nutmeg and cinnamon

Combine all the ingredients in a sealable bag. When it is time to make breakfast, mix everything with 1 cup of water, and soak for about half an hour. After that, put it over heat, and simmer for another five to ten minutes.

Corn and Potato Chowder

This rich chowder does not take long to cook and is filling.

- ½ cup dried corn kernels
- ¼ cup dried potato pieces, chopped small
- ¼ cup dried milk powder
- 3 Tbsp. dried celery slices
- 3 Tbsp. dried sweet potato pieces, chopped small
- ¼ tsp. thyme
- ⅛ tsp. paprika
- Salt and pepper to taste

Mix everything together before you go, and pack in a sealed bag. To prepare, add 2 cups of water to the entire mixture and let it sit for 20 to 25 minutes. Then put it over heat, and bring to a boil. Turn the heat down, and simmer for 15 more minutes until everything is cooked and tender.

Chicken à la King

If you are not drying your own meat, you can buy dried chicken (camping and outdoor stores will have it) or carry a can of chicken meat to add after the rest has cooked.

- ¼ cup dried chicken meat
- 3 Tbsp. each, dried onion, dried mushrooms, dried carrot, dried green peas
- 2 Tbsp. dried milk powder
- 2 Tbsp. flour
- ¼ cup dried thyme
- ⅛ cup dry mustard

If you are using dried meat, everything can be mixed together and sealed in a bag. With canned chicken, combine everything else, and keep the can separate (to be opened on the trail). To prepare, mix all the dry ingredients in 1 ½ cups of water, and soak for half an hour. Then heat to a simmer for 15 minutes. Canned chicken can be added about ten minutes before it is ready so the meat can heat through.

Spicy Tomato Couscous

Couscous is a small type of pasta that cooks quickly and works well in trail mixes. It can be bought at most supermarkets, either with the grains or the pasta. Also, TVP is a dry meat substitute that can be used to replace ground beef in most recipes.

- ¾ cup dry couscous
- ¼ cup dried tomato pieces
- ¼ cup dried hamburger (or TVP)
- 2 Tbsp. dried onion pieces
- 1 Tbsp. dried chives
- 1 Tbsp. dried parsley
- 2 tsp. beef bouillon powder
- ½ tsp cumin
- ½ tsp garlic
- ⅛ tsp black pepper
- A sprinkle of red pepper flakes (optional)

Store everything together, and keep in a packable container. To make, heat 1 ½ cups of water to a good rolling boil, and then pour over all the ingredients. Cover, and let sit for about ten minutes. Give it a stir, and eat.

Trail Colcannon

This one is named after a traditional Irish dish of potatoes and cabbage. It is a nice change from the more typical trail food.

- ¾ cup instant mashed potato flakes
- 2 Tbsp. dried milk powder
- 2 Tbsp. bacon bits (the shelf-stable type)
- 3 Tbsp. dried cabbage pieces
- 1 Tbsp. dried onion
- 1 tsp. dried parsley
- ½ tsp black pepper

All the ingredients can be mixed and stored together in a plastic bag or other container. Boil about 1 ¼ cups of water, and then stir in the ingredients. Simmer for a few minutes, and then remove from heat. Cover up the pot, and let it sit for about 15 minutes. Stir to fluff up the potatoes, and serve.

Mediterranean Couscous

This is another recipe using couscous, so it cooks fast. This recipe makes up just one serving so you can double it (or triple it) if you are cooking for a group.

- ⅓ cup couscous
- 4 Tbsp. dried chicken pieces
- 2 Tbsp. dried artichoke
- 2 Tbsp. dried peas
- 1 Tbsp. dried tomato pieces
- 1 tsp. Italian seasoning spices
- 1 tsp. bouillon powder (chicken or vegetable)

Combine everything, and store in a bag for transport. To make, add enough boiling hot water to cover all the ingredients, and let it sit covered until everything has softened up. Stir to loosen up the couscous, and eat.

Trail Coleslaw

This dehydrated side dish needs to be made with fresh ingredients and then dried. It goes well with just about any meal.

- 1 Tbsp. canning salt
- 1 cup water
- ½ head of cabbage, shredded
- 1 stalk celery, grated
- 1 carrot, grated
- ½ large green pepper, shredded
- ¾ cup vinegar
- 1 tsp. mustard seed
- ½ tsp. celery seed
- 1 cup sugar

In a bowl, combine salt and water. Soak cabbage pieces for an hour, then add in the other vegetables for an additional 20 minutes of soaking. Drain and rinse everything.

In a small saucepan, combine the rest of the ingredients. Pour the dressing over the vegetables, and toss to cover. Let it marinate overnight in the refrigerator. Drain off the excess liquid and spread the coleslaw on your dehydrator trays or on trays in your oven.

In a dehydrator, dry at 120 F for about 12 to 14 hours (18 to 20 in the oven). Because of the sugar, you should not dry this outdoors in the sun. Once it is dry and crispy, you can package it to take on the trail. To make your coleslaw, soak in equal parts water for half an hour. It should not need to simmer.

Peach Cobbler

You can make a tasty and simple dessert for the trail without having to resort to doing any campfire baking.

- ½ cup dried peach slices
- ¼ cup bread crumbs
- 3 tsp. sugar
- Dash of nutmeg and cinnamon

To pack this mix for the trail, put the peach slices in one bag and the other ingredients in another. Sugar can sometimes have some moisture to it, which is why it should be stored separate from the fruit slices. To make dessert, combine the contents of both bags in a small pot, and simmer in ½ cup of water until the peaches are soft.

Drink Mixes

Dry mixes can be used to make drinks as well, although most of these ingredients are not what you would be drying at home. But if you are drying milk, you can make use of that with these recipes.

Hot Cocoa Mix

This good, basic make-ahead mix can be whipped up into a cup of hot cocoa in minutes.

- 2 cups dry milk powder
- ¾ cup sugar
- ½ cup cocoa powder
- ½ cup powdered non-dairy coffee creamer

If you do not have coffee creamer, just use an additional ½ cup of milk powder. Use a whisk to blend all the ingredients together and store in an airtight container. To prepare, add 3 or 4 tablespoons of the mix to 1 cup of boiling water. Mix well until everything dissolves.

Instant Cappuccino

This will not create the foamy coffee-shop version, but it is a nice coffee-flavored hot chocolate.

- 1 cup chocolate milk powder
- ¾ cup dry milk powder
- ½ cup instant coffee crystals
- ½ tsp. cinnamon
- ½ tsp. nutmeg
- ⅛ tsp. ground cloves (optional)

Whisk everything together, and store in a tight container. To make, use 1 or 2 tablespoons in each cup of boiling water. Stir well before drinking.

Apple Mulling Spices

This recipe is a spice mix you can use when making mulled wine or spiced apple cider.

- 3 oz. cinnamon sticks
- 5 whole nutmegs
- $\frac{1}{3}$ cup dried orange peel, chopped
- $\frac{1}{3}$ cup dried lemon peel, chopped
- ¼ cup dried apple pieces, diced
- ¼ cup whole cloves
- 1 Tbsp. dried ginger, minced

Put the cinnamon sticks and nutmegs in a small plastic bag, and whack them with a rolling pin to break up. Then combine with everything else. To use the mixture, wrap about 2 or 3 tablespoons of it in cheesecloth. Heat wine or apple cider in a cooking pot until simmering, and add the spice bag. Let simmer for half an hour, and then serve hot. The bag of spices can be tossed out.

Baking Mixes

You can save a lot of time by preparing all the dry ingredients for your baking ahead of time. These mixes also make nice gifts (make sure to include the instructions). Just keep in mind that nearly all recipes will require an addition of milk, egg, and/or butter when it comes time to bake.

Sweet Cherry Cookies

These simple cookies are packed with fruit.

For the mix:

- 1 ¼ cup flour
- ½ cup whole rolled oats
- ½ tsp. baking soda
- ½ tsp. salt
- ⅓ cup brown sugar
- ⅓ cup white sugar
- ½ cup dried cranberries
- ½ cup dried cherries
- ½ cup chocolate chips

To prepare:

- ½ cup butter, soft
- 1 egg
- 1 tsp. vanilla extract

Preheat oven to 350 F.

In a small mixing bowl, mix the butter and egg. Pour the dry mix into a larger bowl, and then stir in the butter and egg mixture. Mix until everything is moist and well combined. Drop large spoonfuls of batter on a greased baking sheet. Bake for about ten minutes or until the edges start to turn brown.

Oatmeal Fruit Cookies

This recipe is another baking use for some of your dried fruit. These chewy cookies have a lot of fiber as well as fruit in them.

For the mix:

- ½ cup brown sugar
- ¼ cup white sugar
- ¾ cup wheat germ
- 1 cup quick oats
- ½ cup dried cherries
- ½ cup dried apricots, chopped
- ¼ cup raisins
- ½ cup dried coconut
- 1 cup flour
- ½ tsp. baking soda
- ½ tsp. salt

To prepare:

- ½ cup butter, soft
- 1 egg
- ¼ cup milk
- 1 tsp. vanilla extract

Combine all the mix ingredients together, and store in a closed container until you are ready to bake. When baking, first preheat your oven to 350 F.

Pour all the dry ingredients into a large mixing bowl, and stir to make sure everything is well combined. Add the soft butter and work through with your hands until it is moist. In another small bowl, beat egg, milk, and vanilla together, and then add this to the main bowl. Stir thoroughly, and then drop spoonfuls onto a cookie sheet (they will spread; so leave an inch or two between them). Bake for ten to 12 minutes.

Tropical Fruit Muffins

Not all dry mixes have to be for cookies. You can make lovely muffins with this recipe and adjust the fruit as you like.

For the mix:
- 2 ½ cups flour
- 2 tsp. baking powder
- 2 tsp. cinnamon
- 2 tsp. allspice
- ½ cup chopped nuts
- ¼ cup dried pineapple, chopped
- ¼ cup dried mango, chopped
- ¼ cup dried banana, chopped
- ½ cup dark brown sugar

To prepare:
- 2 eggs, lightly beaten
- 1 cup milk
- ½ cup butter, melted

Preheat oven to 375 F.

Mix all the dry ingredients together, and then add all the wet ingredients to the bowl. Stir until you have a batter, then pour out into your muffin tin. Bake for about 20 minutes or until a toothpick in the middle comes out clean. It will make about 12 muffins.

CASE STUDY:
PEPPERS —
TOO HOT TO HANDLE

Jim Willis
Theodosia MO 65761

Jim Willis has been dehydrating food for more than five years and currently is using one of the large 9-tray Excalibur units to do all of his food-drying chores.

His focus is on retaining the nutrients in his food, and so he keeps his dehydrator to a lower temperature (105 F). The lower temperature prevents any enzyme losses due to the heat. Jim even uses his dehydrator to create a raw vegetable lasagna using flat slices of zucchini instead of noodles. Once made up, he dries it just long enough to take out the excess moisture for a "less soupy" dish.

For the most part, Jim uses his dehydrator to create quick soup mixes and meal dishes as well as to save food for the long term. Once dried, his foods go into tightly lidded glass jars. He also uses vacuum sealing to create meal-sized packages.

The most popular foods to dry around Jim's house are tomatoes, basil, and peppers that he uses to create a quick soup base to save time when cooking later. He has never had much luck with eggplant though. It always seems to come out rubbery for him.

One particularly notable session involved a load of hot peppers. He had to move the entire dehydrator to a more open room than the kitchen because the fumes were so bad. When it came time to grind the dried peppers up for powder, he was wearing a face mask.

Eventually, Jim wants to try creating granola crackers, dried for long-term storage. He says his recipe for them involves a lot of prep work so he just has not gotten to them yet.

Chapter 13

COOKING
RAW FOOD WITH
A DEHYDRATOR

This chapter may seem like a strange contradiction, but this concept is gaining ground as a popular use for dehydrators. The term is a little misleading, as food is not actually cooked this way. It is still a close approximation of this technique though.

The whole premise is that eating raw food is healthier than eating cooked food because heat destroys so many enzymes, proteins, and other chemicals in our food. So, many people have "gone raw" and no longer eat any cooked food. However, they do use dehydrators to "cook" certain foods, providing that their food is not heated beyond 110 F. The low heat and drying action can be used to make cookies, crackers, and a number of other foods that end up similar to cooked food. It is the only way to make a crisp or chewy food without cooking.

Raw food also means any processed ingredients that have been heated are eliminated, such as white sugar. If you are doing any raw food cooking with a dehydrator, you will need a sizeable collection of ingredients that may seem unusual at first. Of course, if you are already eating raw, you probably have all these things on hand anyway.

Although these recipes might not be to everyone's taste, they certainly show off the wide potential of the simple food dehydrator. You definitely can do more with it than just dry food.

Recipes for Making Raw Food

Most of these recipes are using soft doughs or liquid batters, which do not work that well with the regular slotted trays in a dehydrator. If you are going to try these, you will need to have nonstick

Photo courtesy of Douglas and Sherri Brown

sheets used for making fruit leather. Most dehydrators come with them, or you can buy them separately. Wax paper would do in any case.

Although you sometimes can use dried foods in these recipes, they are designed to be made with fresh fruits and vegetables. They need the extra liquid in the fresh foods to make the proper consistency. If you were using dried foods to start with, these would be too dry to make proper dough.

When making crackers, you can either make a large sheet of them to be broken up later or wait until they are partly dried and use a knife or pastry cutting wheel to score the drying dough to make more even cracker shapes.

Oatmeal Raisin Cookies

As oatmeal is not considered raw, this recipe has been adapted to use quinoa instead. Quinoa (pronounced keen-wa) is a healthy grain.

Quinoa

- 1 cup quinoa
- 1 cup pecans
- ½ cup agave syrup (a natural raw sweetener)
- 1 cup raisins
- 2 tsp. cinnamon

You need to start this recipe the night before. Give the quinoa a good rinse with cold water, then leave to soak overnight. Drain off any excess water when you are ready to make your cookies.

Use a food processor to grind the nuts until they are powdered. Add in the cinnamon and then the soaked quinoa. Run the processor for about another 30 seconds before adding the agave syrup to the mixture. Keep blending for another minute.

Remove the canister from your food processor, and stir in the raisins by hand.

Drop spoonfuls of dough on either wax paper or the leather sheets that come with your dehydrator. You can place them pretty close together because they will not spread like traditional cooked cookies do. Flatten them out a little, so they are all the same thickness (more or less).

Run your dehydrator at 105 F for four hours. Take them out, remove the cookies from their sheets, and place them directly on the mesh trays of the dehydrator. Keep on drying for another four to five hours.

Mexican Flax Crackers

This recipe makes a zesty and flavorful cracker that takes nearly no time to prepare before putting it in the dehydrator.

- 3 cloves garlic
- 1 small onion
- 1 stalk celery
- 2 carrots
- ¾ cup raw pumpkin seeds
- 5 cups flax seeds
- 3 small tomatoes
- 1 red bell pepper
- 1 small bunch of fresh cilantro
- 2 Tbsp. taco spices
- ½ tsp. ground cumin
- ½ tsp. salt
- 2 Tbsp. lemon juice
- 2 Tbsp. lime juice

Soak the pumpkin seeds overnight before you start making your crackers.

When ready to start, roughly chop the vegetables, and then put all the ingredients into your food processor. Blend until pureed, and then spread on your nonstick leather sheets in your dehydrator. Dry like you would a fruit leather except have the dehydrator turned down to 105 F. Dry for six to eight hours, then peel each piece from the sheet, and flip it over. Keep drying for another six to eight hours until it is dry and hard. Break up into cracker-sized pieces to eat.

Potato Crisps

This is a simple recipe and would be enjoyed by anyone, raw enthusiast or not. You can season these any way you like.

- 2 large white potatoes
- ½ cup cider vinegar
- ½ small onion, minced

The seasonings can be anything you want, such as dried dill, garlic, chili powder, cilantro, or just plain salt. The amount can be between a teaspoon and a tablespoon, depending on how zesty you like your potatoes.

To make these, you need to grate or shred your potatoes and let them soak in vinegar overnight. The next day, drain the potato, and give it a quick rinse. Dry it off with paper towel as much as you can, and then stir in the onions and whatever seasonings you wish.

Spread the potato mixture evenly and no thicker than a ¼ inch on your nonstick leather sheets. Dry at 110 F for about 14 to 16 hours. Part way through, you can flip pieces over to dry evenly. When done, you should have a crisp sheet of potato to be broken up into snack size pieces.

Zucchini Corn Wraps

These soft wraps are similar to leather and can be used when making all kinds of things instead of tortillas.

- 2 cups corn kernels

- 3 small zucchini, peeled and diced
- ½ cup water

Combine everything in a blender, and process until smooth. Spread out on leather sheets in a thin layer, and let dry at 110 F for six hours. Flip the pieces over, and dry for another two hours. They will be slightly crisp when they are done, but when they cool outside of the dehydrator, they will soften to the right consistency.

Apricot and Cashew Cookies

You can change the fruit in these if you wish, but apricots do go well with the cashews.

- 2 cups cashew nuts
- 1 cup dried apricots
- 1 cup raisins
- 2 very ripe bananas

Start this recipe the night before, and let your cashews soak in water overnight. The next day, blend everything until you have a crumbled "batter." Drop spoonfuls on your leather sheets or wax paper and dry at 105 F. Dry for ten hours on one side; then flip them over, and dry until they are firm and chewy (likely another six to eight hours).

Lemon Cookies

These are only lightly flavored with lemon, so they are sweet rather than tart. The banana adds a mellow touch and makes these delicious.

- 2 cups cashew nuts
- ½ cup lemon juice

- ½ banana
- ¼ cup honey
- ⅓ cup agave syrup
- 2 cups dried shredded coconut
- 1 tsp. vanilla extract

Soak cashews for about four hours (overnight will be too long), and then drain them thoroughly. Combine the ingredients and blend in a food processor until smooth. Drop spoonfuls of batter onto your dehydrator nonstick sheet, and dry at 115 F for about eight hours. Flatten them to about ½ inch thickness once they start to dry to help keep things even.

Chocolate Chip Cookies

To keep this recipe strictly raw, you will need to use raw oats, which can be hard to find. Cacao nibs are also a bit exotic, though many bulk food stores carry them. An easier option is to use traditional rolled oats and regular chocolate chips instead if you are not following a strict raw diet.

- 1 cup zucchini puree
- ⅓ cup agave syrup
- ½ cup coconut butter
- 1 cup oat flour
- 1 ¼ cups rolled oats
- ½ cup cocoa powder
- 1 tsp. ground cinnamon
- ½ cup walnuts or pecans, chopped
- ½ cup cacao nibs

In a food processor, blend zucchini puree, agave, and coconut butter until smoothly combined. In another bowl, stir the oat flour, cocoa powder, and cinnamon together, and then add the wet ingredients to the bowl. Stir in the rolled oats, nuts, and cacao nibs. Mix until you have a good batter and everything is mixed.

Put spoonfuls on a dehydrator sheet, and dry at 115 F for about six or seven hours until you have a chewy cookie.

Chewy Banana Bites

These treats are a mix of sweet fruit and crunchy seeds.

- 4 bananas
- 2 cups almonds
- ½ cup flax seeds
- 2 Tbsp. sesame seeds
- 10 large dates
- 1 tsp. ground cinnamon
- 1 tsp. vanilla extract

Soak both the almonds and the flax seeds overnight before you start this recipe. Drain the nuts, and then mix them with the other ingredients in a blender or food processor. Blend until you have a chunky batter.

Drop spoonfuls on a nonstick sheet, and dry at 110 F for about eight hours. If you like them chewier, then continue to dry your cookies until they are the consistency you prefer.

Veggie Chips

These make a healthy alternative to crackers or potato chips. You can be creative with the vegetables and adjust this recipe to suit what you have on hand.

- 1 small onion
- 2 stalks celery
- 1 small bell pepper (green or red)

- 1 tomato
- 1 large carrot
- ½ cup green peas
- ½ cup sesame seeds
- ½ cup corn kernels
- Seasonings to your own taste

These can be seasoned with garlic, basil, chili, dill, or whatever you like. How much you use will depend on the spice; so, plan to experiment a little bit.

Combine everything in the food processor, and run until you have a thick and chunky mixture. Spread thinly on a leather sheet and dry at 105 F for about eight to ten hours or until crisp. Break up the pieces into bite-sized chunks, or cut into squares while drying.

Cheez-It Crackers

There is no cheese in these crackers, but the spicy taste is a lot like the commercial cheese crackers you can buy in stores.

- 1 cup sunflower seeds
- 1 cup almonds
- 1 cup Brazil nuts
- 1 small tomato, chopped
- 1 red bell pepper, chopped
- ¼ cup ground flax seed
- 1 tsp. cumin
- 1 tsp. salt
- 1 tsp. onion powder
- 1 tsp. garlic powder
- 1 Tbsp. taco seasoning mix

Soak seeds and nuts for about four hours, and then drain any excess water. Combine the nuts and everything else in a food processor until it is a smooth batter. Spread thinly on a fruit leather sheet or wax paper. Dry at 110 F for ten to 12 hours or until your crackers are dry and crispy.

Falafel

If you are not familiar with it, traditional falafel is a food made with a chickpea paste that is then deep-fried to make it crispy on the outside. It is a popular food among vegetarians, and you can make a good copy of it with your dehydrator.

- 1 cup chickpeas (also known as garbanzo beans)
- 1 cup sunflower seed
- 1 Tbsp. garlic, mince
- 2 cups fresh cilantro, chopped
- ½ cup tahini (sesame paste)
- 1 Tbsp. salt
- ½ cup onion, chopped
- ½ cup lemon juice
- ½ cup olive oil
- 1 ½ tsp. cumin

You can either use canned chickpeas (not strictly raw) or soak your beans overnight. Either way, drain off any excess water, and then mix the beans together with everything else in a food processor. When you have a good paste going, form into balls, and press flat onto your dehydrator sheets. Dry them at 90 F for around eight hours. The outside will be crunchy, but the inside will still be moist.

Soaking and Drying Nuts

This is not a recipe as much as it is a technique that raw food enthusiasts use to improve the nutritional quality of their raw nuts.

Nuts of all types have some natural compounds in them that make them somewhat hard to digest. It is not great for your body and can give some people stomach upsets when they eat too many raw nuts. So, you can soak your nuts (typically overnight) or give them a good rinsing to remove all the unwanted enzyme inhibitor and then dehydrate them to make them crunchy again. The result is a crunchy nut without the enzyme problem.

To dry soaked nuts, set your dehydrator at 110 F, and then dry until the nuts have re-crisped. If you are not concerned about them remaining truly raw, you can turn the temperature up to 120 F for a quicker process. It will take at least 12 hours to redry your nuts, and it can take up to 20 hours. Small seeds such as sunflower seeds or pumpkin seeds also can be soaked and dried this way. They take six to eight hours to redry after soaking.

This usually is done with raw nuts, but even roasted ones can benefit from a soak and rinse as well.

Chapter 14

CRAFTS AND OTHER USES

Your dehydrator can be a versatile assistance in the kitchen and can be used for many additional tasks besides drying and "cooking" food. With a little creativity, you can find many other uses for these handy machines.

Making Pet Treats

Sticking with food for the moment, one other path you can take with a dehydrator is to make healthy (and inexpensive) treats for your pets. The simplest pet treats are just regular dried meat, usually the cuts that do not work as well for human consumption when dried.

Liver, gizzards, or heart make excellent treats. But any dehydrated meat will work as a pet treat.

Unlike meat dried for your own use, you do not have to cook meat before drying if it is being used for animal treats. Slice raw meat thinly, and let dry at around 140 F for ten to 12 hours.

If you want to try your hand at something a little more sophisticated, you can try some of these recipes for more gourmet treats for your dogs or cats.

Chicken and Liver Treats for Cats

This is one recipe specifically for cats, though dogs usually like them, too.

- 1 lb. ground chicken meat
- ¼ cup liver, minced or ground up
- ½ cup powdered milk
- ¼ cup chicken broth

Combine everything, and mix until smooth. Use nonstick leather sheets, and spread out the mixture evenly. Dry at 150 F for eight to ten hours until they are hard.

Meat and Rice Treats for Dogs

The kale in this is not necessary, but it does add a hefty nutrition boost for your dog.

- ½ cup cooked rice
- ½ cup chicken broth
- 2 Tbsp. dried kale, crumbled
- 1 lb. ground beef
- ½ cup dried Parmesan cheese

Mix all ingredients together, and let sit for about an hour before you start drying. Use wax paper or a nonstick sheet for drying. Spread it out about ¼ inch thick, and dry for eight hours at 150 F.

Vegetarian Dog Treats

Not all pet treats have to have meat in them. If you prefer not handling meat in your dehydrator, this is a good recipe to try. Even though they are meatless, these are perfectly healthy for dogs, and they love them.

- 2 ½ cups flour
- ¾ cup dried milk powder
- ½ cup vegetable oil
- 2 Tbsp. brown sugar
- ½ cup shredded carrot and/or apples
- 1 egg
- 2 bouillon cubes (vegetable or beef)
- ¾ cup hot water

In a small bowl, dissolve the bouillon in water, and then mix that together with all the other ingredients. Mix until you have stiff dough, and roll out to about ¼ inch in thickness. Use a cookie cutter (or even just the edge of a drinking glass) to cut out treat shapes, and place them in your dehydrator. A finer mesh screen or even a nonstick sheet may work better than your regular trays for this.

Dry at a high temperature (about 150 F) for about eight hours. When done, the treats should be hard and crisp.

Another popular vegetarian option is dehydrated sweet potato. *See Chapter 6 for more on how to prepare this.* Slices of dried sweet potato are rich, sweet, and great for dogs.

Drying Flowers

Using dried flowers for flower arranging, potpourri, or other crafts can be a challenge if you do not have a good source for dried flowers. If you have access to fresh flowers (either purchased or right from your garden), you can produce excellent quality  dried material for any use. Once dried, flowers will last years without any problems with insects or mold.

Any kind of flower or plant can be dried in a dehydrator. Whole blossoms can be dried as is, or you can pluck petals off first if you want them for potpourri. Leaves also can be dried if you wish. Remember they will shrink and shrivel once they dry, so do not expect your flowers to look like they did going into the dehydrator.

As they dry, some types of flowers and plant material might release their seeds or pollen, which can make a bit of a mess. There is not much you can do about it, but cover the table that your dehydrator is on with a cloth, just in case.

Not all flowers will dry the same. Set your dehydrator to about 100 F, and check your flowers after about four hours. Most individual petals would be done by this point, but larger or fleshier flowers will not be. They might take as long as 12 hours. Unlike food, you do not have to be quite as precise with flowers. Once they are papery or crisp to the touch, they are dry enough.

You do not necessarily have to have a separate unit or trays for flowers, but you should always wash the trays off well before using your dehydrator again with food.

Once dried, most flowers will lose a lot of their aroma. If you are drying to make potpourri, you usually have to add some scented oils to the mix of plant material to create an aromatic mixture. Flowers do not come out of the dehydrator smelling like a bouquet of fresh blooms.

Helping with Crafts

Drying flowers is not the only area where a little extra drying power can help in the craft department.

Anything made out of clay or craft dough can be put in a dehydrator to speed up the drying. Flat items can be dried in a stacking-type unit, but otherwise this would only work with a cabinet machine with the trays removed. Painted items can have their drying sped up this way. If you are building small items, a dehydrator can help glue dry more quickly as well.

Papermaking is another unique way you can put your dehydrator to use. Making your own paper involves using a blender to puree a mix of shredded paper and water. This is then spread out on mesh sheets to drain and finally dry into new sheets of paper. Laying out the pulp on dehydrator trays and letting it dry this way will speed things up dramatically. You probably should use paper towels while you do this, as the paper pulp can be drippy at the beginning.

Humidifying

Last, you can use your dehydrator to add a little moisture to the air. Just put some shallow dishes of water on your trays, and let it run for a few hours. It actually can do a good job at this if you do not want to have a separate machine for humidifying.

To take this one step further, add a little cinnamon or vanilla extract to the water, and you can add some pleasant smells while you moisten the air. It is a nice touch in the house during the winter.

Conclusion

Dehydrating is a wonderful way to save fresh foods when they are in season, and it also represents a return to an older and simpler way of doing things. You can preserve a huge variety of foods, even with the simplest (and cheapest) of dehydrators. If you harness the sun for your dehydrating, it can be a very environmentally friendly approach as well.

Whether you are drying to preserve your own harvest, to create lightweight camping foods, or to save money with store-bought produce, you now have all the information you need to be successful at it. It will take a little practice to develop the right eye to tell when dry foods are ready, but experience is a great teacher.

Though some topics included in this book are not ideal for beginners (such as trying to dry dairy products or meat), you should be well on your way, even if you have never dried food before.

Bibliography

AllRecipes. **www.allrecipes.com**.

Backpacking Chef.com. **www.backpackingchef.com**.

Ball Blue Book: Guide to Home Canning, Freezing and Dehydration. Indiana: Altrista Corporation, 1998.

Bell, Mary. *Food Drying with an Attitude.* New York: Skyhorse Publishing, 2008.

Bills, Jay and Shirley. *Dehydrating Food: A Beginners Guide.* New York: Skyhorse Publishing, 2010.

Dehydrator Book. **www.dehydratorbook.com**.

DeLong, Deanna. *How to Dry Foods: The Most Complete Guide to Drying Foods at Home.* New York: Penguin Books, 2006.

"Do Vegetables Retain Nutrition When Dehydrated?" *Livestrong. com.* **www.livestrong.com/article/340307-do-vegetables-retain-nutrition-when-dehydrated**.

Emery, Carla. *Encyclopedia of Country Living, Ninth edition.* Seattle, Washington: Sasquatch Books, 1998.

Fodor, Eben. *Solar Food Dryer*. British Columbia, Canada: New Society Publishers, 2006.

"From SAD to RAW." **www.fromsadtoraw.com**.

Greene, Janet, Ruth Hertzberg, and Beatrice Vaughan. *Putting Food By, 4th edition*. New York, 1991.

Hobson, Phyllis. *Making & Using Dried Foods*. Massachusetts: Storey Publishing, 1994.

Layton, Peggy. *Emergency Food Storage & Survival Handbook*. New York: Clarkson Potter, 2002.

MacKenzie, Jennifer, Jay Nutt, and Don Mercer. *Dehydrator Bible*. Toronto, Canada: Robert Rose Inc., 2009.

Author Biography

Terri is living on five rural acres and slowly building it into a thriving farm with large fruit and vegetable gardens. Though she grew up in the city, today she prefers a natural country life with her significant other and young daughter. By managing a freelance writing career from home, she can spend most of her time outdoors tending to both garden and livestock, which has given her a great deal of hands-on experience that she treasures. The need to preserve the annual harvest is always a challenge.

Not only has she gleaned her knowledge from experience but also from the numerous helpful neighbors who seem to constantly have tips and suggestions to offer. Eventually, Terri hopes to be more self-sufficient to produce and preserve most of her own food. When not in the garden or barnyard, she studies genealogy and collects antique typewriters.

Index